WEAPONS OF SELF DESTRUCTION

John and Nancy Banks-Lear

Dedicated to our precious children,

Alexander John and Holly Louise, who have already set out so strongly on their own career journey and in a short space of time are already climbing quickly upwards towards their lofty goals, dreams and ambitions.

We believe in each of you totally and we know that there is nothing you cannot accomplish once you set your mind to it!

Never doubt yourselves.

God bless.

WEAPONS OF SELF DESTRUCTION

The complete upwardly mobile management guide

Chapter 1. All about you

Chapter 2. Default settings and governments in power

Chapter 3. The power of words

Chapter 4. Thought and action

Chapter 5. Thought and manifestation

Chapter 6. A true story...How do you see yourself?

Chapter 7. Manager types

Chapter 8. From No 67 to No 1 in less than a year!

Chapter 9. The personal 'credit' account

Chapter 10. Assertion

Chapter 11. The Success Calibration

Chapter 12. All about business

Chapter 13 Goal setting

FOREWORD

Why did we decide to entitle this book Weapons Of Self Destruction?

Over the years we have delivered seminars to over 300,000 delegates at convention centres throughout Europe and during this time we have chatted to thousands of people, listened to multitudes of challenges both personal and business that they faced, given advice when asked, and eventually we came to this realisation: Most people do not understand how they 'work' and in consequence, at worst, they unwittingly destroy any chance of success they may have had, and at best, they diminish their chance of a place at the top table...How?

By unconsciously using weapons of destruction... against *themselves*... hence the title, Weapons Of Self Destruction!

In this book we will expose these weapons and explain how they work and how to eradicate them completely, so that they can no longer prevent you from reaching that glittering prize...your place at the very top. Not only that, but we will be addressing the key issues of management so that by the time you've finished this book, you should have an in-depth understanding not only of how to get the very best from yourself, but also any business or organisation that you manage.

Every year, tens of thousands of young people stand at the edge of a vast plain called a 'career in management' and gaze into the distance.

Very few will look with total and absolute confidence at the 40 or so years that it will take for them to cross that plain and believe that by that time, they will be wealthy and successful and will have reached the very top of the 'success mountain' that is shrouded in mist on the distant horizon!

Those with little or no imagination, if they look to tomorrow at all, see no danger, risk or threat, however most aspirant managers gaze into the distance with varying degrees of fear, trepidation...and a flush of adrenaline!

The wildebeest, or gnu, as it is often known, that must make the journey through the sweltering heat of the vast African plains every year in search of fresh grazing, must learn very quickly about the dangers and threats that lurk behind virtually every scrub bush, rock and river crossing, just waiting to catch out the unwary. Those that learn the lessons very quickly survive and thrive, those that don't, soon fall victim and become dinner for something else!

Some may consider that this simile is somewhat unrealistic when applied to a career in management in today's World. They may believe that the harsh days of "corporate dog eat dog" have passed, and that we now live in more enlightened times.

Well, here's a word to the wise.

Please remember two things; first that the African plains are littered with the horned skulls of wildebeest who mistakenly thought the same, and second, that human nature today is still exactly the same as it has always been since the dawn of time, and events through history show that it is dominated by ego and greed.

This is not some kind of paranoia because I am not suggesting for a minute that every boss, colleague and associate you will ever work with will be ego driven, motivated by greed and consumed with jealousy, or that they harbour a secret desire to stitch you up at the drop of a hat, but be warned...some will. The problem is that the majority of people wear a mask so you may not know who is that way disposed until you feel the knife in your back!

Remember also that behind the mask they are pursuing their own agenda which may not be the one they show on the outside.

So, is this book some kind of corporate infighter's survival guide?

No, most certainly not!

Our aim is not only to explain how to get consistent peak performance from yourself and those who work with you, but also about how to interpret and manage those Key Performance Indicators (KPIs) that make the difference between a healthy business and a sickly one just months away from being on the skids. We will not only mix in some essential corporate jungle survival skills, but along the way we will explain how to deal with those 'difficult' people both above and below you on the ladder!

At this point we will assume that you are either contemplating a career in management or have already embarked upon one and are wondering why your progress is so slow, and it matters not if that career is involved in the manufacture of widgets, the selling of services or the retailing of goods, because the issues we shall be discussing here in this book are applicable to management in *any* environment.

We must also not forget those entrepreneurs who have taken the plunge, started in business and have now reached the point where their business has grown to the extent that they are employing more and more people and controlling more and more resources. This book is also for them because in order to expand and survive they must now learn to 'manage'.

Our guiding methodology in how the information will be presented is based on the 'KISS' principle, which stands for: Keep It Simple, Stupid.

Also, where we use the word 'he' or 'she' except in specific terms, we mean either he or she!

CHAPTER 1.

ALL ABOUT YOU

First, let's define what management actually is before we go any further. There are several dictionaries and encyclopdias from which to gain a definition, however we consider that Wikipedia has a very complete definition of the term management, and it may be found at : http://en.wikipedia.org/wiki/Management

Management in all business and organisational activities is the act of coordinating the efforts of people to accomplish desired goals and objectives using available resources efficiently and effectively. Management comprises planning, organising, staffing, leading, directing, and controlling an organisation (a group of one or more people or entities) or effort for the purpose of accomplishing a goal. Resourcing encompasses the deployment and manipulation of human resources, financial resources, technological resources, and natural resources.

Since organisations can be viewed as systems, management can also be defined as human action, including design, to facilitate the

11

production of useful outcomes from a system. This view opens the opportunity to 'manage' oneself, a prerequisite to attempting to manage others.'

Interesting isn't it, that the final sentence states that managing *oneself* is a prerequisite to managing others, in fact Confucious who was born over 500 years BC, said 'He who conquers himself is the mightiest warrior, so to begin with we will focus on *you* as an individual, since we know that the most difficult of all people to manage... is one's *self!*

Once we have discussed *you* in some detail and given you the steer to help you become top management *potential*, we will go on to discuss *you* in the context of applied management and then we will finish up discussing the pure management skills that will help you to effectively and profitably manage your business or enterprise.

So, beginning with *you*, let us explain in an analogy what we call the 'Government In Power' principle.

It's 5.20pm on Monday and as people begin to pack up and leave the office, Jim pipes up and says, 'Tell you what guys, did you know that on Friday, Gladys in accounts has been here for 25 years? Yeah, I was chatting to Karen in Personnel about it earlier today, and we decided it would be nice to all meet up at the Green Bowman at 7.30pm for a drink and give her a little present. We're only talking about a fiver to sign her card and 7.30pm should give us all time to get home, changed and back by then. What do think?'

Your government in power at 5.25pm on Monday considers the invitation, a free vote is taken by your mental parliament and it is agreed you will go.

'Yeah, that's fine, count me in, I'll defo be there.' You confidently reply as you walk out of the office.

Tuesday passes, Wednesday passes and you don't think much about Gladys and the Green Bowman. Thursday dawns and in the parliament of your mind, the Opposition, have been mumbling and grumbling about having to come back on Friday evening.

13

During Thursday night the Opposition tabled a motion that you should not attend.

On Friday morning the floor of your mental parliament is filled with shouts, bleats, hoots and boos as the Opposition begin crank up in support of their motion to backslide on the arrangement to go to the 25th anniversary celebration.

The leader of the Opposition, the Meganeg Party, is the Rt. Hon Mr Morbid Misery who rises to take the Despatch Box and he delivers a rousing speech highlighting that it is, after all, Friday night! He states that you spend enough time at the office, that you deserve to have some fun, that it's Friday and that you could be out on the town with some girl or other...and as the piece de resistance... he reminds you that you *hate* Gladys for telling your boss about a mistake you made in your last sales projection when she could have told *you* instead, the old bitch!

To the accompaniment of screeches and jeers, the leader of your Government, The Rt Hon Mr Can Do of the

Rambo Party rises to defend the policy, appealing to the House's sense of fair play and honour.

A free vote is taken, the Meganegs win and it is decided that you won't be attending after all.

You get hold of Jim as soon as you arrive at the office and tell him some lies about something that has come up, that you will cough up the fiver and sign the card, but that you won't make the Green Bowman at 7.30pm.

Monday arrives and you hear your colleagues discussing what a great success Friday night had been.

You can't join in, you weren't there.

You learn to your dismay that it was attended by none other than the Managing Director himself, Mr Arrowsmith! He spoke to everyone and apparently spent at least 20 minutes at the bar in close conversation with Jason, your competitor for the promotion you are after!

Once more a debate is raging in your mental government, this time dominated by Mr Can Do who delivers a harsh, 'I told you so, I hope you are pleased with yourself, it could have been you talking to the MD to push yourself forward for promotion, but no, you had to give in to the child in you and go and have some fun instead didn't you? When will you ever learn?'

After the harangue from the leader of the Rambo Party you feel totally hacked off for not *taking firm control of your* self, for not being strong, and for not making yourself do what you know in your heart you should have done instead of weakly giving in to what the child in you persuaded you to do instead!

Silly little allegory, but it illustrates the point about how hard it can sometimes be to control 'self,' or put another way to make sure the *right* Government stays in power come what may!

Since it is you who will be making that once in a lifetime journey as you progress your management career, we think it would be a good idea to create a solid foundation on which to build your future as a highly effective manager, so we'll start with *you*.

To begin with let's understand that we each have a mental 'government' in power 24 hours a day, 7 days a week that controls our thoughts and in turn our habits and actions; thoughts, habits and actions that will determine the level of success that we will achieve as we journey over the vast plain of years that is our career.

It is *essential* that we develop a mental government that is of the correct political 'colour' if we are to have any chance of succeeding during those 40 or so years we will spend on our career plain en route to that high mountain peak of success that lies shrouded in mist far in the distance.

35 years of age is a good number to aim for, give or take 5 years or so either side of it, by which time to get to the top, so if you are a young 25 year old with your feet on the first rungs of management, you should be seriously expecting to get into the top team during the next 10 years. That allows for the guys above you now to pop off to retire thereby creating the space for you to move into...and no, I don't mean that you should be content

to wait to move into dead man's shoes, not at all. Once you feel competent in your current position and have had that competence recognised by a good appraisal or two perhaps, if your present company cannot map out a reasonably fast career track for you, then you need to start to look outside.

Be warned however, nobody wants to waste money by investing in a 'job hopper,' so give it at least two to three years with credible reasons for moving on!

CHAPTER 2.

DEFAULT SETTINGS AND GOVERNMENTS IN POWER

As you will be responsible for your own success in management, let's begin with *you* and explain in some detail about our earlier reference to 'governments in power.'

Why do you think the title of this book is 'Weapons of SELF destruction?'

Well, we agree it's a play on the words used to frighten us all a few years ago about what turned out to be the imaginary threat posed by Saddam Hussein in Iraq!

So many people completely *self* destroy any chance of the success they might have achieved by simply not understanding the workings of that wonderful machine, their brain, and how to develop and use it effectively to get what they want from life because instead, completely oblivious, they use it as a weapon *against* themselves that then prevents them from succeeding!

The good news is that it is simply not necessary to have a degree in order to succeed. As evidence we need look no further than people like Richard Branson, founder of the Virgin empire, who is dyslexic, or Henry Ford who left school at 14 and went on to build one of the most successful motor manufacturing companies ever, or good old Alan Sugar who came from a rough area of London...on the other hand we know that the World is littered with educated derelicts.

Average intelligence, *correctly* applied, is all you need in order to succeed!

All success in any field of endeavour comes first with thinking the right thoughts in the right way, second, by developing the right habits, third by doing the right things at the right time, and fourth by applying consistent effort in the right direction until the objective is achieved.

Please accept that your journey to success over that vast plain of your career may *not* be air-sprung and fur lined. Like the dear old gnu, you will experience times that are great, when the grass is green and plentiful, times when it is scarce and belts must be tightened, and of course there will be times when the rivers must be crossed and the crocodiles must be faced!

On your journey you must develop what we call mental toughness, persistence through a total commitment to achieving your goals and objectives. However...and this may seem a total contradiction to what has just been said, you will find as you look around that some people seem to glide easily and effortlessly up the promotion ladder to the top with apparently little effort!

Do these people know something that the rest don't know? Yes they do actually, but don't worry; we will share this information with you as we go through this book so that you can benefit from it as well...as long as you use the knowledge of course!

Default Settings and Mental Governments.

Earlier, we gave a silly but accurate analogy of the workings of mental governments in our mental parliament, showing that unless we ensure that we vote the *right* government in to power and make sure we keep it there, we cannot hope to succeed. I never use the word 'cannot' lightly since it is a negative, however I must use it in this context because it is so obviously true; success cannot be achieved by a government whose policy is all about failure!

Let's drill down and discuss all about mental governments.

The mental government that is predominantly in power is determined by what we call our 'default setting.' It is very important to understand what our own default setting is, how we got it and how it determines the shade of the government we have in power, and of course in turn, ultimately the degree to which it will either help or hinder us in our own journey through life.

We are all familiar with the default settings on our computer. Consider the default you have set for the font that Microsoft Word uses when producing your documents. It could be the Arial font for example.

Whenever you open up a new Word doc, *by default* as you type, the text will appear using the Arial font. You will *never* see your computer suddenly decide to produce a page full of Copperplate Gothic instead!

Quick question...How did Arial *become* the default setting on your computer? The answer is...surprise, surprise... is that *you* set it that way!

Now let's move into the default setting of your mental government!

As we have said, the default setting determines the 'shade' of our mental government and in consequence the response that we habitually make to certain situations, opportunities and threats that arise. For example; suppose that whenever someone comes to you and starts to complain about their life and some difficult situations they are facing, your natural reaction (default setting) could be to say 'Oh dear, you poor thing, come and tell me all about it.' So then you put your arm around their shoulder and listen to all their woes and offer comfort and support.

23

The perfect default setting for those working in the Care industry of course, but perhaps not quite so perfect for the role of Operations Director who would need to empathise in certain situations, but never to sympathise!

On the other hand, your natural response (default setting) to such a situation could be to react by saying 'Oh dear, what a shame, how bad, too sad, come on, get a life! Compared with those poor people in XYZ land who just had that massive typhoon where thousands have lost their lives, your situation is a bed of roses, so come on pull yourself together and get on with it!'

What about a situation where the business needs all the stops pulling out and a major effort made to achieve a seriously big objective that will tax you virtually to breaking point?

When the boss calls you in and tells you what is required, your mouth agrees, but privately the government in power is screaming out the very opposite...'That's a ridiculous demand to make! Stupid bitch! How am I possibly going to be able to convince

24

my staff to do that when our hours have been cut and I'm already one down through pregnancy...They just won't be able to do it, it's a complete waste of time. Oh well, she's the boss so we'll have to go through the motions anyway just to keep her happy.'

An alternative government in power, when confronted with the same challenge however, would begin to think about how to achieve the objective despite being down on hours and with one short through pregnancy. It would come up with solutions, it would look at all the alternatives, it would see what 'favours' it could call in to help, it would have a team meeting, it would be charismatic in how it promoted the objective, it would set goals for each team member, it would promise rewards, it would gain commitment, it would tell the team that it believed in them and motivate them by selling them the idea that together they were going to make it happen... end of discussion!

If you were the boss, which of those governments would you like to have in power in the minds of your management team? The right answer is pretty obvious!

We all know people who can walk into a gathering and the room temperature drops 10 degrees and everyone wants to leave, conversely we all know people who can quite literally brighten up the whole room... question is, what makes the difference? The answer is their default setting!

Once more, which default setting would be most useful to you?

Before we go any further, you must look inside yourself and decide what your own default setting actually is. Perhaps, given that we often tend to delude ourselves, it might be a good idea to involve someone who knows you well...Remember; we do not see ourselves as others see us!

Let's see where your default setting came from, *how* it became your default setting, *who* set it and then, if it isn't the kind of default setting that will put the right mental government in power, how we can go about changing it for one that will help you succeed in your management career.

Imagine that a new born baby's brain is like a computer that has not yet been programmed with any software beyond its basic operating system. As the baby begins to experience life it begins to receive its mental programming in the form of 'downloads'. Initially these come from its parents, but as it begins to experience more freedom and grow into adolescence and then adulthood, it also begins to receive programming from influential adults and life experiences. Into this category fall teachers, employers, line managers, husbands, wives, partners, influential friends and many others who interact with us as we journey through life.

Now as well as programming from others, the new person also begins to 'download' programmes from its own life experiences. For example the child may once have stolen some change that was lying around for

27

example, and when it was challenged about this, it learned that if it admitted the theft then this would automatically lead to an unpleasant confrontation and so, because of *that* painful experience, built in to the individual's default setting is now the natural reaction in those kind of circumstances to lie in order to try and avoid the confrontation...Parents, consider this!

As the individual reached adulthood he or she may have become romantically involved with another person and then been betrayed, leading to the new default setting which tells them never to trust another man/woman ever again!

Perhaps they bought a car and believed all they were told by the salesman, who just happened to forget to tell them about a serious defect that did not emerge until the MOT was due! Yet another experience of life has been racked up that teaches them to beware of salesmen and never to believe a word they say in future!

This type of situation applies to many, many things in life, and it is called 'life experience.' It is life experience

28

that continually contributes to the default setting we have and in turn the government in power that determines whether we succeed or fail!

Most damage is done to our default setting during our early years and it is done by parents who just did not understand what they were doing when they told us things like, 'You are *so* clumsy Sarah!' when we spilled our juice on the carpet, or 'Jason, you are the laziest person I know!'

There is some really powerful negative programming out there that is delivered as compulsory downloads to children by their misguided parents, teachers and contemporaries. Below is a small selection that will help you get the flavour:

'You are so stupid!'

'You will never be able to do that!'

'You're absolutely useless. You're a complete waste of space!'

'What did you do that for, you stupid little twat!'

'You will never amount to anything, you are an absolute idiot!'

'Don't get your hopes up; people like us never get anywhere!'

'You are so ugly; nobody would ever want to go out with you!'

'You've got freckles; your sister is far prettier than you!'

'You are fat and stupid!'

'Don't bother to apply; you'll never be able to get that job.'

The examples given above are extreme and have been used only to graphically illustrate the point. We could go on endlessly with other less severe but equally damaging examples, but we're sure you get the picture!

An individual who suffers years of a mix of that kind of mental download is hardly going to have a good self-image and will certainly find it very hard to achieve anything with their lives, because download by download their default has gradually been set and in turn a mental government programmed for failure has been confirmed for life.

Those who have suffered more than just a little of this type of download *must* fail...by default...just as the most expensive and powerful computer will fail if it is infected with a virus!

How this might be lived out is when the individual is looking for a job for example!As they scan the adverts the mental conversation goes like this, 'Oh, that looks interesting. Maybe I could do that job, mmm, the pay is OK. But then the mental government suddenly kicks in and shouts, 'No, you'll just be wasting your time, all you'll get is another no. You aren't good enough, so just forget it!'

I'm sure we have all met people in the course of our work that we see as very capable, but somehow doing a very menial job, and we wonder why. The most likely reason is that *they* do not see themselves as worthy of anything better due to their low self- esteem...brought about by? Yes, a lifetime of negative downloads that created their default setting and in turn their government in power, which delivered the results expected!

They have in fact become a self-fulfilling prophecy!

Let me give you a real life example. We recently went to the home of friends who are loving and well-meaning parents, but who just did not understand the consequences of the negative downloads with which they were infecting their child. We arrived at the house and as they opened the door their son Jason was standing between them and he was introduced to us like this: Ruffling his hair they said, 'This is Jason, you're a little imp aren't you Jase?' 'We call him Terror Tot; he's always on the go. Don't know where he gets the energy from, never sits still for a minute, do you Jase?'

The outcome? Very predictable of course, because it became a self-fulfilling prophecy that evening! Poor Jason was duty bound to *prove* his parents right and so he put on the most *amazing* performance of racing around like a lunatic, climbing over his parents, pulling their cheeks as they were trying to talk to us and of course they smiled benignly at their progeny who then stoutly resisted going to bed. Then they said, 'Told you he was an imp, didn't we! Told you he wouldn't go to bed!' Wow, what a surprise!!

My private thoughts were 'Numpty, you *made* him that way!' If only they had downloaded other programming, perhaps telling Jason that he was always a very good boy, a good boy who always helped his mummy and daddy, who always went to bed at bedtime, then I guess the outcome of the evening may have been rather different!

I always laugh to myself when I see those misguided mums who put the stickers on the rear window of their car that say 'Naughty Little Person On Board.' In our view they deserve the nightmare journeys they undoubtedly get!

We brought our two children up with totally the opposite programming to that illustrated above. We never delivered a negative download, only highly positive downloads that shaped their default settings and in consequence their mental government. What do we have today? Two young adults of whom we are intensely proud who both are in very significant positions within their companies, and who are moving up the corporate ladder at a great speed!

This book is not intended to be a treatise on how to bring up children, and we have included this information only to illustrate how our default settings are constructed and the consequences of allowing an unhelpful one to determine the shade of our mental government and ultimately our quality of life.

We included it also because it is an *essential* component in understanding how your mind works, why it works in the way that it does and how to make sure the right mental government is always in power which will become the best helper you'll ever have as you make your journey through your career in management.

Quote: 'You are what you think you are.'

CHAPTER 3.

THE POWER OF WORDS.

As you move on in your management career and as you strive to ensure the right mental government is always in power, it will become important for you to be able to spot people in your team who may not have the 'right' mental government and who may not be fully committed to achieving the objectives you personally strive for, although they may pretend otherwise.

If you listen carefully to the everyday conversation of the people around you, you will soon find that they give away their mental programme, their default setting and the shade of their government in power by the word clusters they use.

To illustrate this with a true, but extreme real life example, let me introduce Bill; Bill was a next door neighbour we were once 'blessed' with, whom I tried to avoid like the plague to the degree that I used to look round the corner before I dared step out onto the driveway!

If I did get caught, I had to work very hard not to let him vomit his mental garbage all over me and I always did my level best to get away as soon as possible....An urgent meeting that I was running late for saved me many times!

'Oh, hi John, how are you doing?' Before I could answer he would launch into 'Just look at that...just cleaned the flipping thing yesterday...blooming bird shit...why did I buy a dark blue car!'

'I'm just off to take Sally out for a run....had a terrible night with her last night...never slept a wink...she's got cancer you know...oh yes...been hell! Can't even think where we can go today...been here for 32 years now you know...been everywhere round here. Oh I'm so fed up. Did you hear that motorbike last night? Oh you probable didn't, your wife wasn't keeping you awake at 3 in the morning was she?'... And on and on and on and on!

After 10 minutes with Bill you begin to think life just isn't worth living!

This is a prime example of the topics and the word clusters Bill normally used, clearly indicating his default setting and the shade of his government in power.

Instead, why couldn't he be grateful that there were no clouds in the sky on that beautiful spring morning? Grateful that his wife was still alive, that he had a nice new car and another God given day that they could share together and the time to go out somewhere nice in the new car together?

Keep away from people like Bill. They will not only bring you down by affecting your own attitude, but their negative attitudes will also infect others they work with. Imagine having the likes of Bill in your team!

We mentioned earlier that some people just seem to effortlessly glide through a highly successful management career, whilst others struggle and slog and find it hard to move up even a single rung in 10 years! In our experience only 20% of people have a relatively smooth path upwards, whilst 80%, to a greater or lesser extent, have to struggle.

Why?

Well the heading of this section is: The Power Of Words and you may be surprised that a greater part of the success of the 80% group is down to understanding and using the power of words.

Let's look at some of the issues. You will never in a million years hear members of the 20% group use words in the way Bill uses them, conversely you will find many members of the 80% group habitually doing so to a greater or lesser extent.

The 20% group would never allow failure words like 'can't' and 'try' to pervade their vocabulary, neither would their conversation be dominated by gossip, or running other people down, or complaining, or criticising, or condemning or by negatively comparing.

These topics are common ground for many 80%ers.

We hope that we have clearly proved that the words and therefore the thoughts of the 20% group are starkly different from those of most of the 80% group and this

39

is precisely what creates the difference in status between members of the two groups, their levels of success and ultimately their earnings.

Whilst we're on the subject of the two failure words stated above, it is best to remember that success comes in 'cans' and failure in 'cant's'. We also mentioned the word 'try', and I recall that when our children, Alex and Holly, were small, we tippexed out the word 'try' from our dictionary!

When we heard either of them say that they would 'try' to do something...we would say...'try? What a funny word, what does it mean?'

They would reply 'Don't be silly daddy, you know what it means!' To which we would reply, 'Well every word that ever there was is in the dictionary isn't it? So go and look it up and see if you can find it and tell us what it means!'

Off they would trot to the study and come back minutes later and say 'It isn't there daddy,' holding the dictionary up as evidence!

Then we would tell them the story of Luke Skywalker of Star Wars fame who somehow crashed his spacecraft into the swamp when he was on a mission to rescue Princess Leia.

He was in despair and Yoda, the little guy with the big ears who had been teaching him how to lift rocks with his mind for several days, tells him he is now ready to raise the spacecraft out of the swamp in the same way, by using the power of his mind.

Luke looks at him dumbfounded, and replies, 'I'll try!'

Yoda shakes his head and utters that immortal line, 'There is do or do not, there is no *try*!'

That proved the point to them, and after that they resolved to *do* and never to *try*!

Which came first, the chicken or the egg?

No easy answer to that one, here's a simpler question: What came first, the thought or the word?

Well, except for those who open their mouths before they put their brain in gear, the correct answer is that the thought came first and then provoked the word.

However, for the most part our thoughts rarely provoke words. When you are alone thoughts fill your mind, but unless you have a little mental problem, you don't go around muttering and expressing them verbally. They remain unspoken words!

Most people's minds are filled with mental chatter every hour they are awake, sometimes focussed on a task or a conversation, but for most of the time our minds drift from one thing to another. It might be a good idea to make a note to self to sit down later on and see if you can remember what you have been thinking for the last 10 minutes. We are certain that unless you have been thinking about something specific, something you are doing or must do, you either won't be able to remember or the thoughts will have been just idle chatter!

That is a good reason to sit down quietly at some point during every day, to relax and clear your mind and to meditate! Yes we do suggest that brief meditation in a quiet place is a very helpful process that will help clear your mind of irrelevant chatter and make it more effective in reaching decisions. No, you don't need to sit cross legged, arms outstretched with thumb and forefinger touching whilst you chant a rhythmic 'Ommmm' sound!

CHAPTER 4.

THOUGHT AND ACTION

So, we all agree that the thought came before the word. Now we need to delve a little deeper into the thought aspect of our minds to understand *how* we think and the consequences of *what* we think, and how this will impact upon whether we struggle and struggle and never really succeed as one of the 80% group, or glide fairly effortlessly along to success as one of the 20% group.

What we're going to explain next is the *main* key to your ability to succeed, so best get some coffee before you start!

We will go back to when we were first here on the Earth to show by analogy the distinct element of the process so we will be able to understand more clearly how thought and action interact so closely to help us succeed...or cause us to fail...then we will get to the nuts and bolts!

Quick note to start with.

Ever wondered what it was that saved us from extinction back in those dinosaur days when we had no armour plated scales or sharp teeth and claws to protect us as other creatures did?

The answer is...we had something that none of the others had...a highly developed forebrain.

Below is a simple example of how we used this wonderful forebrain way back then and we have continued to use it in basically the same manner ever since. It has been responsible for every technical advance and innovation the Human Race has ever made since the dawn of time!

Suppose you were a primitive cave dweller and one day you were out searching for food. Your search took you into woodland, and there you had to pick your way over some fallen trees and thick undergrowth. As you do this, you trip over something and sprawl flat on your face!

You get up and quite naturally turn round to see what it was that tripped you. There you see a long branch that has fallen from a tree.

At that point in time you had 3 choices: Curse the thing, rub your shins and move on. Pick it up, curse the thing and break it over your knee...or pick it up and study it. Let's suppose you decided to pick it up and study it, but before we continue, first let us give you some words from Albert Einstein that will help you understand what is going to happen as you do this.

"Imagination is everything. It is the preview of life's coming attractions."
Albert Einstein (14 March 1879 – 18 April 1955)

So you pick up the piece of wood, you hold it in your hand, you see that it is straight, you see that one end is thicker than the other, and finally you see that the thick end, where the branch broke off, is sharp to the touch.

Imagination kicks in. You balance it in your hand, you raise it above your head, you aim it at a tree 20 metres away and you hurl it with all your might. It flies to the tree, hits the trunk and falls to the ground. You walk over to it and run your hand over the gash in the bark and your eyes take on a distant look!

Now, in your imagination, it is no longer a deep gash in a tree trunk, now it is a deep gash in the side of a wild pig... and the rest is history!

You now see that with this stick you will not only be able to hunt down animals that are faster than you, but that you will also be able to protect yourself from predators who would eat you!

You then set about perfecting the tip so that it was very sharp and you broke off the bits of twig still attached to it.

Over millennia this 'stick' underwent an amazing evolution until it became a primary weapon of war used to great effect by the Greeks and later the Romans, the javelin!

So, what was the process?

First it was our *imagination,* made possible by our highly developed forebrain. This gave us the idea, next we made it our *intention* to manifest the idea into reality, and then we gave it our *attention* to make it so, once more, courtesy of that fantastic forebrain!

So the steps are:

Imagination > intention >attention > make it so.

Enter into the equation...The Universe!

Imagine a Neanderthal suddenly transported from his cave and into your home here in the 21st Century! He would be completely oblivious to the invisible energy that flows through your home in the form of electricity. He would be completely unaware of this invisible energy, invisible, yet powerful enough to kill him! Energy that flows constantly and silently, energy that is in harmony with the laws of physics. Yet it is only ignorance that prevents him using this powerful force to light up a room, provide heat, or boil water, and all at the flick of a switch.

Remember, at home he would first have to gather wood and light a fire in order to do all those things.

He *could* access this invisible powerful energy in your home if he knew of it and actually *believed* it existed. We imagine you would have a pretty hard job attempting to explain the principles of electricity to him. If instead, however, you had helped him overcome his fear and actually try it by stretching out his hand, touching the switch with his finger and then turning the light on, he would then be able to accept that electricity actually *is* even though he did not understand *how* it *is*!

Now it must be plainly obvious that if only he would accept that electricity *is* and would learn *how* to switch *on* a connection into it, then he would begin to *use* it to his benefit.

So what has this got to do with you, the aspiring young manager?

Well, remember the 20% and the 80% groups and how one group struggles and the other doesn't seem to get it anything like as hard as they progress on their journey across that vast plain of their career?

Remember we told you that the 20% group know something the others don't know?

Well this is it!

In the same way that the Neanderthal is ignorant of the power of electricity, the vast majority of people in the World today are completely oblivious to an 'umbilical' connection that they have to a form of energy, a universal power that is far more potent than electricity, an energy that surrounds them in every dimension. A universal power, an omnipresent, omnipotent universal energy by which and through which all things are connected, and through which is manifest all things that ever were, are, and ever will be. A fundamental energy that complies with ancient immutable laws, so ancient yet so advanced that luminaries like Steven Hawking, the outstanding British scientist, have only just begun to identify and understand them!

As electricity *is*, universal power also *is*, and just because the Neanderthal in our story did not initially believe electricity *is*, this lack of belief did not make electricity *not*.

It is absolutely *essential for your success* that you understand the information contained in the following two sentences!

1. The fact that you may *not* accept that universal power *is*, will not in any way diminish its power to create or destroy in your life, only your ability to use it to your positive benefit should you choose to do so.

2. The fact is that universal power will still be working in response to the data that you unconsciously transmit to it 24 hours a day, 365 days a year, through your umbilical connection to it; *even though you may not believe it exists.*

Understand this.

The data that gets unconsciously transmitted to universal power originates from our government in power…which, remember, gets it's 'policies' from your default setting, so this is the path of the connection: default setting > government in power > content and quality of the data transmitted > quality of manifested result.

To explain this a little more fully, let's go back to the fable of Aladdin, who if you remember, found what turned out to be a magic lamp? As Aladdin picked up this dusty old lamp he studied it closely and then, because it was so dirty, he began to rub it clean. Suddenly, as he rubbed, out of the spout emerged this massive genie that towered above him and asked what he wanted before booming out, 'Your wish is my command!' The Genie then went on to give Aladdin everything he asked for!

That, dear reader is *exactly* how your connection with universal power works!

That is the good news, and sadly it is also the bad news, but first let us explain the precise mechanism by which universal power works so you fully understand why it is both good and bad news!

Remember default settings and how they determine the flavour of the government in power?

Remember the two government parties we used to illustrate the point? The Meganegs, whose leader is Mr Morbid Misery and the Rambos whose leader is Mr Can Do?

These were chosen as two diametrically opposite extremes, however in reality there are different shades between the two, just as shades of grey could be considered the median between black and white.

The government run by Mr Misery will not want you to undertake anything new or, as he perceives it, out of the dull and boring comfort zone they want you to exist in for all of your life. If you should one day have even a glimmer of inspiration they will drag out negative examples from the thousands of items they have on file since you were a baby, examples of when you 'tried' to do something and failed. To these files they will add the voice over echoes of the past, 'You'll never amount to anything, you're stupid, people like us never succeed…' Mr Misery will tell you that you had best forget all about it and just keep doing what you've always done and play it safe…because you will never amount to anything, so what's the point?

What has actually happened is that Mr Misery has planted a creeping doubt that will grow in power in your mind the more you think about it, and as Karim Seddiki said, 'Doubt kills more dreams than failure ever will.'

From William Shakespeare 400 years ago…

'Our doubts are traitors and make us lose the good we oft might win by fearing to attempt.'

So, the solution is plain to see…never doubt yourself!

Its very sad that not many people seem to be able to grasp this so obvious and fundamental point which is that if you keep on thinking the way you have always thought, then you'll keep doing what you've always done, then you'll always have what you've always had...and if you're ok with that then that's fine!

Mr Misery will get you thinking constantly about what you *don't* want and he will make you constantly focus on the things you lack in your life.

You will think thoughts like, 'I've never got enough money, I never get on with my bosses, my friends don't like me, I can never keep a girlfriend, I can never do what I want to do, I'm never really happy with my life.' and sure enough the 'genie' will deliver these things into your reality.

Now here are the nuts and bolts of how those thoughts get sent to universal power and in turn, like the genie, to then become manifest into the reality of your life!

The thought is first conceived in your conscious mind and then because your conscious mind is linked to your subconscious mind, what your conscious mind knows your subconscious minds also knows...but nothing more!

The only way your subconscious can get any information at all is through its connection with your conscious mind. It's rather like living in a prison and getting fed information through one source only, a hole in the door!

Now let's not knock our dear old subconscious, because it really is a fantastically useful device!

Remember when you were learning to drive? You had to *consciously* think of every action that then had to be co-ordinated in order to make the car move.

To begin with you had 'kangaroo juice' and the car jumped and lurched all over the place as you set it in motion...however it wasn't very long before you were able to drive smoothly and it wasn't very long after that that you were able to drive on a motorway for example, and forget where you where!

So who was actually driving the car whilst your mind was far away somewhere else?

Answer?

Your good old subconscious mind of course.

I can still remember learning to fly. My take offs were terrible and my landings worse, such that I thought I would never master the art. Now I can fly along without actually *thinking* of what I'm doing, it just happens...thanks to my wonderful subconscious mind!

Now here's the really interesting bit!

Your subconscious mind actually has another connection as well as the one it has with your conscious mind. From your conscious mind 'data' flows *into* your subconscious mind and from your subconscious mind the same 'data' flows *out* as a transmission down to your solar plexus.

Your solar plexus is a vast ganglion of nerves in the area under your rib cage and it is your solar plexus that in turn has the umbilical connection with universal power through which data is transmitted, thus completing the 'circuit'!

Remember the term, 'gut feeling?'

Where is gut feeling centred? Why, in your gut, aka your solar plexus of course!

It is in this area that you feel all those unexplained sensations that you get about people, places and situations...feelings that you would be best served to take notice of and not over-rule with your conscious mind which is what we all tend to do until we understand!

Fact is, those feelings come from the same source that saved the lives of our distant ancestors when they approached a woodland, or some rocks for example...in which were hidden predators who would have killed them if they hadn't 'listened' to that strange gut feeling and run away!

So the 'system' works like this: Thought created in conscious mind > subconscious mind > solar plexus > universal power> eventually manifests dominant thought into your life's reality.

Anyway, back to the umbilical connection.

It is through this umbilical connection that thoughts are transmitted, for example thoughts like 'I've never got enough money, I'm always broke, I never get on with my bosses, my friends don't really like me, I can never keep a girlfriend, I can never do what I want to do, I'm never really happy with my life.'

Guess what?

The genie, aka universal power, says, 'OK, what was that? Never got enough money, always broke. OK no problem; I'll handle that for you. What was next? Never get on with your bosses, your friends don't like you, you can never keep a girlfriend, you can never do what you want to do and finally, you're never really happy with your life. OK, no problem, as you have spoken so it shall be done, your wish is my command!'

And so *you* have brought the lack into your own life...*you* have constantly focussed on what you *don't want* and not what you *do* want...hence the title, Weapons Of **Self** Destruction!

On the other hand, if instead you had Mr Can Do's party in power, you could think, 'Money always flows to me, I always get new business easily, people always like me when we first meet, my business is growing fast year on year, people always want to do business with me and money always flows to me.'

Guess what the genie says and guess what happens next?

That's a bit simplistic, but that IS just about the way it happens!

An interesting point to raise at this stage: We constantly research unexplained human experiential phenomena and have found that many answers lie in pre-history, perhaps because that period of time is closer to the time when the 'gods,' or aliens apparently visited Earth. The study of ancient texts from various civilisations and religions can be quite revealing, take the Biblical story of Job from the Old Testament for example.

In modern parlance, Job was a rich man, a landowner, a farmer, a merchant and an employer of many men. He had a big house filled with beautiful items that he had acquired and over many years he had developed a business which had continually gone from success to success. If the story was told in today's time, he would perhaps have had an Aston Martin in the garage as well as a Mercedes 4x4!

Anyway, he also had a beautiful wife and a beautiful daughter as well and then, for some inexplicable reason, despite the years and years of good harvests, plenty of water to keep his wells full, healthy cattle, fantastic wine production and superb sales...strangely he began to think negative thoughts!

'What if there is a drought, all my crops will fail! What if my cattle get sick and die? What if something happens to my wife, what if my daughter became unwell and died?'

For some unexplained reason he began to withdraw more and more into himself and become more and more depressed.

For some reason he allowed a complete change of his mental government in power to take place, despite the fact that the one he had allowed to govern all his life so far had produced outstanding results over the years. If you will, in his mind the Rambo party was gradually ousted by the Misery party and that is why things began to change; they had to in order to align Job's actual life reality with Misery Party policies which in turn governed Job's thoughts and his data transmission!

So...ultimately all those things came to pass and he lost everything, including his family.

He cried out that famous line, 'For the fear which I feared, hath come upon me: and that which I was afraid of, hath befallen me!'

This is the earliest example we have discovered of the 'speak it into existence' syndrome and its awful consequences...so be careful what you think about. In fact, on that point, we have all heard the term 'self-made man or woman' normally in reference to a wealthy or successful individual. The point is that for the most part *everyone* is self- made, rich or poor, successful or unsuccessful as we shall discover!

Remember, the default setting and the government in power of the people in the 80% group create totally different thoughts from the government of those in the 20% group. Either way, those thoughts then create their reality.

The members of the 20% group *expect* to succeed whilst for the most part those in the 80% group *expect* to fail...so why even bother?

So with that let's look at how the 20% group think, those who expect to succeed.

The same creative process; imagination in the conscious mind > subconscious mind > solar plexus > universal power and finally, manifestation into life existence.

Hypothetical example: On holiday in France, Mr 20% receives an advertising brochure though the door of the villa he has rented. He speaks and reads a little French and establishes that this is a little promo book full of discount vouchers showing tourists where to go to get local money off deals with the vouchers.

'Hmmm.' he thinks. 'Mmm, that's a good idea, what if I did that in *my* local town? I'll look into that as soon as I get back!'

Now if we go back to the spear analogy we see what is happening; imagination, intention, attention, make it so.

Mr 20% has decided that he is going to launch a similar book in his local town back in the UK. He does all the things that need to be done first, like establish the potential demand, what the likely overheads will be, what the price per slot needs to be in order to make a profit, what services and support he will need, then he projects how much profit is in the concept and then projects this forward into a rollout process to other local towns.

Decision made, with great enthusiasm...he is going to do it!

That night with those thoughts in his mind he drifts off to sleep whilst the 'data' is sent off to the genie (universal power) to get on with it to help make it all happen.

Ever had a moment when you were thinking of someone you were planning to contact about something and they then called you out of the blue?

Ever had an occasion when you were in a shop for example chatting to the owner, a stranger, about something, when he dropped out into the conversation that his friend had a business that printed material in *exactly the way* you needed it and gave you the guy's number?

Ever sat in the window seat of an airliner and got chatting to the foreign guy in the middle row when, during the 3 hour flight, it emerged that he had access to an important person in his country who could get you the important introduction you needed there?

For us at least, the answer to all those questions is YES because both of these episodes actually took place!

Question is, how did those people get *put* into our path?

We could have visited a different shop and the guy in the middle row seat on the flight could have pre-booked another seat and never met me. These type of examples are endless, and the fact is that once universal power knows what you want it will be given to you...not perhaps in quite the way you expect it, or at a time when you are ready for it, so you must keep your mind open and your 'antennae' up and take advantage of every opportunity presented to you as it arrives.

Do you know what it feels like to have that wonderful warm glow in the region of your solar plexus when you think about something or someone you like or love?

We hope so, because as you think of those things you want universal power to deliver to you, it is *essential* that you express heartfelt gratitude whilst *concentrating* on that lovely warm feeling you'd have, just as if what you wanted had *already* been delivered to you!

Without gratitude the transaction cannot complete and this will hold back delivery of the things or people you need!

However....now here is a quick point to ponder. If anyone should think, 'I want a red Ferrari!' and expect that, hey presto, at 7am next morning there it is on the drive, full tank, keys in and ready to go!

No, not unless the lottery was involved!

No, we do not become successful overnight and have the wealth that often goes with success, simply because we *become* successful over time just as someone *becomes*

67

an astro-physicist over time and does not just gain the qualification aged 10 overnight!

Someone in stand-up comedy for example, of whom reporters might say, 'He became an overnight success' are wrong. No he didn't! He started in the pubs and clubs; he suffered all the heckling and rejection and learned to rise above it. He constantly perfected his material, he got better and better venues as his fame spread and eventually he got to play in mega venues to an audience of 10,000...and so had *become* successful over a period of time!

Take for example one of Britain's most successful stand-up comedians, Michael Macintyre. When he first started he sold just one single ticket to his show at the Edinburgh Festival. Imagine that, how awful must he have felt? It obviously did not deter him, just as well because he sold half a million tickets on his last tour and he sold 1.4 million copies of his 'Hello Wembley' DVD!

It goes to prove the old adage: Winners never quit and quitters never win.'

By what process did he achieve this?

Yes... Imagination > Intention > Attention > Make it so....during which time of course, he was under the guidance of the right mental government in power, under the leadership of Mr Can Do, who of course was in connection with universal power which delivered all he needed and he persisted until he *became* one of Britain's top commedians!

Imagine if he had started with a brief flash of imagination and inspiration which was then quickly extinguished by the Misery party who flooded his mind with negative and wore him down with endless recordings from the past, such as 'You'll never do anything with your life, you're useless, forget it, it's not for you, if you go on the stage the audience will boo and jeer you off!'

We have learned that both the 80% and the 20% groups used universal power to manifest their current life existence, which is why we say that for the most part *everyone* is self-made, and for the most part they have done it unconsciously and it was done unconsciously, because all communication has been automatically carried out by the government in power in accordance with its default setting via the communication channels we have explained!

The 20% group have a positive default setting which is faithfully reflected by their government in power and so they attract all the positive things they want into their lives, whilst the other group, through pure ignorance, unconsciously allow the negative 'default' setting of their government in power to be in control during the automatic communication process, so this in turn automatically manifests into their lives all the things they *do not* want and so, it is by this means that all lack, discomfort, unhappiness and misery is physically manifested into their lives.

Both become 'self-made' men or women!

You may find this hard to accept, but as we will go on to explain more fully, as long as you have an open mind you will begin to realise that a primal power exists that flows all around us and through us, a power that has delivered into our lives all we have ever asked for in the past and will deliver all we will every ask for in the future.

Once you understand the mechanism and how to consistently apply it, you will be able to accelerate your progress, opportunity will open for you, positive co-incidences will occur, people who can help you will be put in your path and doors will open easily!

You will learn later in the book about 'circles of power' and 'circles of influence' and when you do, please cast your mind back to this chapter because once again you will find that those with a positive expectation and outlook are able to develop a large circle of influence which in turn will power them to success, whereas those who have a negative attitude will find it virtually impossible to develop a circle of influence at all.

We have only been able to skim the surface of this fascinating topic and those who want to know more can contact us through our e-mail, which is given at the end of the book, however for those who want more information now, we have included a chapter briefly explaining the actual mechanism.

CHAPTER 5.

THOUGHT AND MANIFESTATION

Having read in an earlier chapter about default settings and how universal power manifests into our lives the precise reflection of that which has been demanded by our government in power, it would be natural to ponder the mechanism through which these esoteric forces could possibly have brought into our life the things, people, relationships, situations and experiences that exist in our present lives and will exist in our future lives.

As an introduction to this arcane science, we have assembled the following information.

We may wonder how, at one extreme, negative fear-based default settings manifest lack, misery, unhappy experiences, unhappy relationships and the things that people *don't* want into their lives through their government in power, whilst conversely, positive default settings bring about the opposite; abundance, happiness, joy, pleasant experiences, happy loving relationships and all the good things that really enhance the quality of our lives and the very experience of living.

Now we are not saying that if you get up in the morning and run round the garden singing happy songs and throwing flower petals over your head that nothing unpleasant will ever happen to you and that you will live a 'Pollyanna' life filled with the song of little birds and the sweet fragrance of flowers! No, absolutely not, however we *are* saying that the potential to enjoy positive experiences in your life will increase whilst the incidence of negative ones will diminish once your thinking changes.

You may wonder how it can possibly be that people with a negative default setting can become so used to negative experiences in their lives that they can go around saying things like, 'See, told you so, look at that…didn't I tell you? Nothing good *ever* happens to me.' Well, you need to believe it because it is perfectly true, they are telling the *actual* truth of their lives; that nothing good ever happens to them!

We now need to begin to understand exactly *why* this is the case, exactly *why* it happens, but also more importantly, *how* it happens and the dynamics that cause it. This is however an extremely complex subject and as we stated previously, if you seriously want to know more of the details, then best e-mail us! In the meantime for the purpose of offering a more reasoned explanation as an aid to understanding, we'll skim the surface sufficiently deeply to put a little 'meat on the bones' of this subject.

To fully understand, you'd have to rush out and enrol for a crash course in quantum physics at your local University and study quarks and bosons and perhaps, just for good measure, the String Field Theory! Now whilst we cannot possibly explain matters quite at the Steven Hawking level, we do hope to give you sufficient information to allow you to understand some of the issues so that you will be able at least to understand the process by which our jolly old default setting brings about the reality of our lives!

Let's begin with a solid object. Why don't you pick up the nearest solid object to you at the moment and hold it in your hand; could be your coffee mug, something made of solid metal, a small rock even. Now hold that item in your hand, feel its surface, weigh it is your hand. If possible wrap your fingers around it as hard as you can....not the mug as it could shatter!

Take the small rock for example, it feels hard and solid doesn't it? If feels so hard and solid that you know that you cannot possibly crush it in your hand. You may be able to take a hammer and break it, but all that would then happen is that you would have smaller pieces of the same material.

Now the point is that the piece of rock is composed of chemical bonds. If the rock was a lump of limestone for example it would be composed of calcium, carbon and oxygen and expressed as $CaCo_3$, as you may well remember from those happy Wednesday afternoons you spent in old Harry Beaumont's Science Lab when, instead of thinking about chemical formulae you were too busy messing about!

So now we know that this 'solid' piece of rock is made up of three separate elements, calcium, carbon and oxygen that have been bonded in a certain way in order to create limestone.

Looking deeper than that we see that calcium, carbon and oxygen are all composed of atoms, but each has its own unique arrangement of atoms that makes calcium calcium, carbon carbon and oxygen oxygen!

Looking deeper we see that those atoms are comprised of a single nucleus with a cloud of electrons that 'buzz' around the nucleus like miniature planets around a miniature sun! An electron is a negatively charged subatomic particle and it has no components or substructure. So that's as small as we can get with the electron because it is described as an elementary particle with no sub-structure....but how about the nucleus of that atom, can we go even deeper with that?

Yes, looking deeper we see that the nucleus is composed of positively charged protons and negatively charged neutrons....so what next?

In brief, protons and neutrons are comprised of quarks....In fact they are each comprised of 3 quarks and quarks are referred to as being either 'up' quarks or 'down' quarks...No, don't ask me who chose the name 'quark'!!

A proton is composed of 2 up quarks and 1 down quark and some gluons, whilst a neutron is composed of 1 up quark and 2 down quarks and of course some gluons... whatever *they* are!

For now just accept that these quarks are the fundamental constituent of matter....but don't ask us why up quarks and down quarks, because we have no idea.

Funny thing is that because of a phenomenon known as colour confinement, *quarks can never directly observed*...hmm!!

Why the lesson in particle physics?

Simply to prove to you that what you see as 'solid'.... is in fact *not* solid at all....*everything,* including you, is a mass of pulsating matter that *vibrates*...

Ah, there's that word at last...now we're really getting to it!

With the giant strides made in quantum physics in recent years, now at last, we have technology powerful enough to enable our scientists to postulate that there actually *is* a 'Law Of Vibration,' and that everything IS made of vibrating energy and everything actually has a distinct and specific frequency at which it vibrates. In other words, that rock, that lump of metal, that car you drive, that plane that takes you away on holiday....*seems* solid but in reality, it is a mass of the vibrating energy from the elements of which it is composed.

Now we've looked at the micro, let's now look at the macro!

The entire Universe is made up of vibrating matter in the same way, and until recently we have all considered that the 'nothingness of space' is exactly that...a vacuum! However it now seems that even this 'vacuum' is not actually a vacuum at all, but is made up of a mouldable 'plastic' substance!

Now let's look at a human specimen!

Now that we've got this far, I'm sure that you would accept that all of creation is a unique mix of very distinct vibrations, however because we humans do not exist in splendid isolation, our vibrations blend and interact with and on other co-incidental vibrations that are occurring throughout every part of the Universe in which we live...however, as well as the vibration created by the elements of which we are composed, there is another source of vibration that we need to consider; the vibration caused by thought!

Let's now come down to a little bit of basic reality!

I would imagine that everyone reading this book has at some time experienced receiving an unspoken thought from someone who is close to them emotionally. Perhaps you have suddenly thought about someone, and an instant later, and as if by magic, the phone rings and it's *that very person* calling you! I would also imagine that everyone has at some time experienced 'feelings' about a place they were in, whether that place was a building, a hilltop, a cave, a deep valley or even a ship! Perhaps you felt washed over by pleasant loving feelings, feelings of incredible peace, of love and warmth. On the other hand, perhaps you have been to a place where you suddenly felt a malignant brooding presence that washed feelings of deep unhappiness, of disquiet, of discomfort over you, to the extent that you could not wait to leave the place!

Now hang on, let's think about this. Feelings are an expression of *emotion* aren't they? So how come an inanimate object such a cave, or a room for example, can possibly radiate vibrations that 'click' with us, such that in consequence we feel a particular emotion?

Let's see!

My wonderful wife and co-author Nancy and I were visiting a town in the south of England a few years ago with our then small children, Alex and Holly, and for some reason we decided to walk into the parish Church that stood in the centre of the town. We had been to the town before, but we had never been in that particular Church and on that day we had no plans to visit it, we had just been walking round the shops hand in hand with Alex and Holly, and enjoying the late afternoon sun and then, for no reason in particular, we decided to walk into that Church.

Once inside, I was attracted to the stained glass windows behind the altar, and so I ambled off in that direction with Alex, whilst Nancy and Holly went in another direction. A few minutes later Holly called to me to come back, and when I did, I noticed that Nancy was nowhere to be seen!

'Mums had to go outside,' was all Holly could say.

I went out into the sunshine with the children and there I saw Nancy standing facing the wall, head in her hands with tears streaming down her face!

Nancy could not talk for quite a few minutes and so I just held her close, stroking her head and comforting her. When at last she could speak, she explained that at the very instant she had left the entrance area and set foot in the Church proper, she had been completely overwhelmed by a powerful feeling of utter melancholy and deep, deep heart rending sadness, an emotion that she just could not explain, an emotion that had struck right at the core of her being.

When she had gathered her composure again we went to a local hotel and discussed this exceptional event further, but we could come up with no reasonable or rational explanation. A week later we called the local Clergyman and explained what had happened and then he came out with a bombshell!

The Church had been built on the site of an earlier building that had burned to the ground 300 years previously with great loss of life! The powerful emotional vibrations of that devastating event remained powerfully locked within that building and Nancy had received them loud and clear over 300 years later!

As far as we are concerned, because of that very distressing, yet very enlightening experience, we just know that we know that we know about vibrations of this type!

Perhaps you have had similar experiences yourself?

Those latent vibrations are the reason you can go to into a room, where unbeknown to you there has been a conflict earlier in the day. You can feel and sense the tension in the room although those who created those vibrations may have left hours before and there was no one else there when you arrive!

I've attended business meetings in board rooms where, as soon as I walked into the empty room, the atmosphere was such that I felt the air could be cut with a knife....because a previous meeting in the room had been so emotionally charged. It's for the same reason that when house hunting, for example, you can look round a particular property and pronounce it to be either a 'happy' house, or an 'unhappy' house. That's how you can say that you 'picked up' or felt bad vibes from so and so, or such and such a place. The word 'vibes' of course is short for vibrations, and in these cases bad ones, caused by previous negative human tensions!

Insofar as you can pick up the vibrations created by others, *your* vibrations in turn radiate out to affect everything around you, including the environment, people and even animals, and of course those seemingly 'empty' rooms or areas in which you have been. You can perhaps describe these vibrations as the 'invisible energy traces' of previous occupants, (including yourself) all of which serves to reinforce the concept of vibration and the frequency of the vibrations that surround us *in every dimension.*

Some would argue that this is no more than the reading of the body language of two people who have been arguing, but then shut up as soon as another person appears. This may be true in some instances where the people are still there, however this is a simplistic conclusion to reach, since it does not address the tensions we can sense in an *empty* room or space.

So we are human 'transmitters' and 'receivers' who are constantly radiating out our own vibrations on the frequencies on which we subconsciously choose to radiate them, equally we are also receiving stations that enable us to detect and be affected by the vibrations of others.

By now I trust that you will agree that there is some substance to what we have been proposing here because you will all no doubt have your own real life experience to back it up! Let's now look into the issue of how and why our dominant default setting and in turn our government in power determines what manifests into the reality of our lives.

All vibration occurs at a frequency specific to itself, just as deep bass sounds are of a lower frequency than high pitched sounds. We are all familiar with radio frequencies and we know that we need to match our radio receiver to the *precise* frequency of the radio transmitter (radio frequency = vibration) if we are to hear the radio station we have chosen to listen to.

So how does this relate to default settings? Well let's take those unfortunate people who have the 'fail' default setting as their norm as our example. As you have read, and I hope by now also understand and believe, we human beings give out vibrations constantly. We can tell what kind of vibrations they are by how we feel about them as they constantly radiate out into the universe from our solar plexus in the way that we described earlier, and which is home of our 'gut feelings' and our 'intuition'.

So, default setting at 'negative-fail' = failure thoughts = strong failure feelings = failure expectations = vibrations resonating at failure frequency = received loud and clear by universal power = failure results returned... *exactly as ordered and exactly as fully expected!*

Those unfortunates who have these failure default settings radiate out thoughts at a *frequency* which is then automatically received by universal power *at that frequency,* which it then *must* deliver and manifest in correspondence with that *exact* frequency.

Or conversely...

Default setting at 'positive-succeed'= success thoughts = strong success feelings = success expectations = vibrations at success frequency = received loud and clear by universal power = success results returned *exactly as expected!*

To be certain of this crucial point please understand that all feelings are in total concordance, and resonate perfectly, with the associated vibration.

Rage vibrates at rage, hatred vibrates at hatred, jealousy vibrates at jealousy, love vibrates at love, calm vibrates at calm, peace vibrates at peace, and goodwill vibrates at goodwill. 'I'm sick of being broke', vibrates at 'I'm sick of being broke', whilst conversely, 'money always flows to me vibrates at 'money always flows to me.'

Guess what? Either condition then becomes ultimately manifested into the thinker and feeler's reality....after its own image!

This is why it is not possible to achieve wealth, health, happiness or love if we simply ask the universe to deliver them...if we are not truly vibrating at those frequencies, but just pretending we are by blindly uttering mere words (sounds) without the corresponding emotional feeling which produces the corresponding vibration.

This is why it is a grave error to wish ill of others...the universe will not allow you to direct its power, and instead the ill you wish upon another will visit you, because you called it down upon yourself!

So many people work hard to achieve results by focusing externally, whilst failing to realise that success must first be achieved on the *inside* before it can be manifest on the *outside,* (your life's reality).

89

Remember the old saying 'birds of a feather flock together'? Based on this aphorism, consider your thoughts and their corresponding vibrational frequency. Failure thoughts, negative thoughts, will attract to you more negative thoughts like vultures around a rotting carcass and the more that land, the more *powerfully magnified* will be the negatively destructive vibrations that they collectively transmit...all to be faithfully fulfilled by the universe which will manifest into your reality of course!!

Equally, positive, uplifting success thoughts will also attract after their like, just as myriads of beautiful butterflies are attracted to the fragrant flowers of buddleia bushes in the summer, and once again the collective power of *their* vibration will bring about the corresponding positive manifestation of abundance into your reality!

In ancient times there was a philosopher called Hermes Tresmegistus. The name Tresmegistus means 'thrice great.'Tresmegistus came up with the Emerald Tablet and an interesting theory which proposed: 'As above, so below', or in other words the Law of Correspondence, the brief details of which we have been discussing here.

Understand this: According to the Law of Correspondence it is *impossible* to have a physical life reality that is different from the 'mental' life reality we hold in our minds.

So the Law of Correspondence requires that we must *first* create in our mind (the above) the things we want to manifest into our lives (the below) in order to achieve them, and this follows the thread of what we have been proposing in this management book.

Thinking about it, the Christian Church's Lord's Prayer actually includes this line; …Thy will be done on Earth (the below) as it is in Heaven (the above).

The point of mentioning this now?

Simply that you cannot expect the results you think you want *if* you constantly think and verbalise thoughts that are at variance with them.

Any incongruity and universal power will tune into the strongest *emotion* and feeling and manifest *that* into your life rather than what you have tried to hold in your mind *intellectually* but not emotionally!

Remember...you are vibrationally and umbilically connected with universal power 24/7!

Remember...like attracts like...what you think *and* feel *will* become your *reality*!

Remember...your life reality will reflect precisely your dominant feelings, because your dominant feelings will control and determine your dominant thoughts and emotions and in turn your dominant vibrations which in turn will determine your life's reality by their data transmission through your solar plexus to universal power!

Now there is something else to throw into the pot; the issue of alignment. There is a constant flow throughout the Universe and the expression 'go with the flow' has rather more depth than the shallow concept most people have of it. It does not just mean 'do what everyone else does,' it means quite literally *go with the flow of Universal energy!*

Let John explain: When I was the Operations Director of a multi million pound organisation, I saw myself as the lantern jawed super hero, Captain Fantastic! A go-getter who could always be relied upon to get things done and make things happen, despite the adversity I might face in doing so. In fact my psychometric test result classified me as 'Mission Impossible.'

If I was told something couldn't be done, my reaction (default setting) would be, 'Oh really? Just get out of the way and watch this space, I'm going to make it happen!'

In other words I spent most of my corporate life swimming against the flow to get what I wanted by *making* it happen. As *I* was going to *make* it happen, I didn't need anyone else to help me and because at that time I most certainly was *not* a people person (Stayed that way until I met Nancy, and she taught me!) I did not appreciate the invaluable benefit of teamwork, often

I utterly exhausted myself in the process simply because I did not understand that all I had to do was *align* myself vibrationally *with* the flow, and once I had aligned myself vibrationally *with* the flow, I could *allow* the things I wanted to happen and things would flow to me with far less effort.

By less effort, I mean that the ideas through which to *manifest* all the things I wanted would flow to me with no effort, however, I would of course still need to physically *do* something about them in order to physically allow them to be manifest into my life's reality.

I now place myself in vibrational alignment and go with the flow and, as if by magic, and with little effort on my part, the situations, the relationships, the resources and the people magically come to me, to help me receive my aligned desire! Notice that word 'receive'? I did not say *get,* we do not *get* anything, we receive. When we receive, it is a *gift,* and when we receive a gift, we must express *heartfelt* (Solar Plexus felt) gratitude to the universe for giving us that gift!

So how does it work?

Well let's expand a little on what we explained in the part about a default setting and a government in power that is set at 'fail.'

That government in power *cannot possibly be* in vibrational alignment with success now can it? So therefore how can an individual who constantly thinks fear based failure thoughts possibly hope to have all good things flow to them? It just *can't* happen any more than they can expect to hear Classic FM when the radio dial is set to Radio 1!

Some people with this particular government in power typically set out to take short cuts, to cheat others, to exploit them so that they themselves can benefit at the expense of others. Once more, this is an example of *wrong thinking* which is *not* in vibrational alignment with the Universe. The consequence is that whilst they may benefit for a while, they will be in constant stress and discomfort because they are vibrationally mis-aligned and this will affect their lives negatively in other ways. Good old fashioned saying, 'Birds come home to roost!'

The Universe is all about growth and improvement and so if your desires are in accord with this, then you will be in perfect vibrational alignment and your needs will be easily met with little struggle.

You picked up this book because you are most certainly intent on becoming a highly successful business manager which in turn will give you the lifestyle you want for yourself and your family, in other words, wealth from success.

Wealth is a balance of an adequate supply of money so that you can do and have the things you want to have and to do and good health so that you can enjoy those things to the full. Wealth also includes good relationships so that you can experience love and share those good things with others....so nothing at all wrong with wishing for wealth, however it is *how* you propose to receive that wealth that *must be in vibrational alignment with the Universe.*

So long as you plan to receive your wealth as a by-product of providing a benefit to others, then your enterprise will be in vibrational alignment and you will receive all that you need to enable you to provide that benefit and enjoy wealth in proportion to the benefit that you deliver to others.

We hope that brief interlude into default settings, governments in power, vibrational alignment and your connection with universal power has been enlightening, let's now turn to something a little more prosaic.

CHAPTER 6.

A TRUE STORY...HOW DO YOU SEE YOURSELF?

A note from the authors:

As John personally handled this assignment, he will tell this true story which we hope will give you some perspective on the range of the issues that we have covered in this book so far and how they affect the ability on an individual to succeed. Incidentally, we've changed the names!

A few years ago I was requested, as a Business Consultant, to sort out a Care Company that was in difficulty and literally months from going under.

The background was this: A woman, we'll call her Judy, had been a Care Worker with a bit of ambition and had decided to leave the 80% group and join the 20% group by working for herself with private clients. As the years went by she added more and more clients and soon she had to employ more and more staff to cope with the demand.

Ultimately she had to get her business formally registered with the Local Authority because she wanted to be able to take on Council funded clients as well as private clients. This of course meant that she then had to comply with reams of paperwork, policies, procedures and a mass of legislation. She did not do too bad a job of coping with this initially, and as the business grew she took on an Office Manager to help her.

Then, for some crazy reason that I never got completely to the bottom of, she decided to relocate 80 miles away, leaving the Office Manager in charge of the business!

Well, without Judy's daily presence, little by little standards began to slip as staff began to take short cuts and spot checks from the Council revealed that legislation was not always being fully complied with which led to her receiving what amounted to a 'final warning.' Clearly, if she wanted her business to survive she would have to do something very significant to get it turned around and then maintain it at an acceptable level.

The only issue was, she had started another Care business in her new home town and so could not leave it to rescue the original business. Enter Darryl!

Darryl was Judy's 30 something year old son. Now unfortunately Darryl had no training in the Care sector at all as his main work experience to date had been a spell in the retail trade on a sales counter followed by a stint in computers and website design.

Clearly these jobs were light years away from a job managing a Care Industry business which, as well as the need to run standard management control systems was also completely tied up in legislation and red tape. As well as these 'system' processes, also included of course was financial management and the most challenging element of all to manage, the human dynamic!

Within this dynamic fell the group of female Care Worker employees who looked after the elderly clients;

Care Workers whose performance level was dragging along at bare minimum. There was neither team spirit, loyalty nor discipline at all within the employee group. Staff went off sick at the drop of a hat, putting intolerable pressure on the others and so staff turnover was high.

A nightmare scenario even for an experienced manager to take on, never mind someone with no management experience whatsoever!

Not only did the performance of the staff leave much to be desired, but the company's financial controls and disciplines were virtually non- existent and since Darryl's nature was to be so laid back that he was horizontal and non-confrontational in the extreme, matters had become much, much worse since his arrival, rather than better as his mother had hoped.

This then was my assignment: Save the business, evaluate the current situation and then put together a programme which would reinstate financial controls, instil discipline once more, develop team spirit amongst the staff and ensure compliance with legislation, review Darryl's performance and then develop him as the manager who would then be competent to run the business effectively after I had gone....all in 6 months!

Dealing with all the pure management issues was no problem to me, after all I had been a Director of a British blue chip company running an operation which employed thousands of staff, however, training someone like Darryl to become an effective manager in 6 months was going to be a very different matter, and it is on this aspect that I want to focus now, because I know that it will be helpful to many who need some guidance to help them become more effective managers.

In fact much of the guidance and training given to Darryl was taken from our management development seminar entitled 'Drum Tight And Razor Sharp' which is designed for managers aiming for the top.

To expand on the background a little more: Judy was a very domineering individual, perhaps she'd had to be as Darryl's father had left them when Darryl was a young child, however the consequence was that she completely dominated him to the degree that he would do nothing unless he spoke to 'Mum' first, and when he needed to tell the staff anything, it was always 'Mum said.' Neither habit contributed anything to the credibility of a 30+ year old 'Manager' and this, coupled with his laid back attitude, made his presence in the office about as significant as a potted plant! He would arrive at the office wearing jeans and a sweat shirt very late in the morning having driven the 80 miles from his home, and he would then leave very early to drive the 80 miles back, having 'popped out' for lunch in the meantime!

So, what to do about it? He seemed a hopeless case!

Listening to the words Darryl continually used gave me a pretty good steer as to his default setting and in turn his government in power. In discussions about how we could improve the business, he would trot out expressions like:

'Yeah, I would have done that...BUT.'

'I wanted to do that....BUT.'

'I could have done that ...BUT...mum said'

The use of the word BUT in contexts like these have always been like a red rag to a bull to me and my natural response is to make clear that the only *butt* is the one the individual is sitting on!

So a major attitudinal change and a root and branch reconstruction of Darryl's default setting and government in power would be required before he would be able to even begin to progress and since, in our view it takes 30 days to develop a new habit and another 30 days to consolidate it, we didn't really have any time to waste!

I considered the situation and decided to use shock tactics to get his complete attention and so I carried out a financial review of the business and then, taking the trends for the previous 6 months I projected these forward for the next 12 months.

The graph I produced showed that the 'deadly cross' would occur in 8 months' time. Now the 'deadly cross' is where the projected blue income line is crossed by the projected red overhead line on a graph and when they do...end of story!

I completed this projection and held my first formal meeting with Darryl. My shock tactics worked, he of course had never attended to financial matters except to look at the bank account and sign cheques. He had never created a Profit and Loss account and knew absolutely nothing about key performance indicators, cashflows, balance sheets, projections or anything else to do with accounting, business management or financial control systems.

When I had finished explaining how the parameters worked, I then told him that he would lose his business the following March, perhaps sooner as the elderly (their clients) tend to die off in greater numbers in the cold months that lay ahead.

I asked him what he thought he ought to do about it and waited for his response. He was silent, looking blankly at the spreadsheet I had given him. Moments passed and I too remained silent, knowing that as long as I did so it would have to be him who would have to break the silence.

I waited.

Eventually he looked up and said, 'Well, I suppose we'll have to ask mum....' to which I responded, 'No Darryl, the buck stops here, YOU are the manager, what are YOU going to do to stop this business failing?'

He had no serious ideas about how we were going to get control of the overhead expenses or how we were going to get more clients in order to generate more income. I knew that I had to get Darryl to start to think for himself and although I had already formulated a business game plan, I remained silent, waiting as he sat looking down at the carpet.

After a few minutes he began to offer up some suggestions, I listened and when he had no more to add, I asked him this question. 'Darryl, do you want the business to fail?' He looked up at me aghast, 'No of course I don't!' I then added 'Ok, you agree that if we just let things continue then that's exactly what will happen, yes? So we need to make some fundamental changes....agree?'

He meekly nodded his head and then I employed what I call the 'sandwich method!'

I told him that he was a really pleasant guy, super personality, good conversationalist, great to have as a friend, however his business was a mirror image of him, slovenly, weak and inefficient and that if he didn't sharpen up he would lose it all, although I knew he had great potential and that with some help he could become a really outstanding success!

That's called the 'sandwich' process and I learned it years ago...it works! Nice > unpleasant message > nice.

He asked me to explain what I meant, and I knew I had hit the mark because he was actually beginning to become a little aggressive as he trotted out the usual loser's excuse…'It's not my fault!'

'Ok, so whose fault is it then?'

His reaction was predictable and he blamed everyone from Amy, the office manager who was 'useless', to the staff who were also 'useless', to his mum who wouldn't listen, to the Council whose regulations were too hard to comply with.

I told him to point his finger at me and say 'It's your fault,' he did so and then I asked him to look at his hand and tell me how many fingers were pointing back at him.

He smirked and answered 'Three'.

'Exactly!' I responded adding, 'there are no such thing as bad staff, only bad managers, so let's get to it.'

'Now if the business folds all your staff including Amy will just go and get a job somewhere else, but what about your mother? This was to be her retirement fund. She worked long and hard to start and develop this business and when it's gone all of those countless unpaid hours she invested, all those miles she drove through all the bad winter weather, all those meeting she had to get involved with at the Council are all going to be a complete waste and whose fault will it be? Come on point that finger at me again...exactly, it will be the fault of the guy who has three fingers pointing back at himself and *that's you sunshine.'*

I followed this up with another harsh point, 'And by the way Darryl, the only place that 'play' comes before 'work' is in the dictionary!'

For a moment he was silent and I thought he was going to cry. He looked up at me and said 'So what shall I do? I don't know what to do, I never asked for this job, I've never managed anything in my life before, I was pushed into it!'

I had been cruel to be kind. If I was to affect a cure, I had to get him to see that he, and he alone was responsible and after I had taken away all his excuses he was naked and had nowhere to hide and it was only at that point that we had got down to the bedrock on which to build the foundation for potential recovery and future growth.

I asked him to make some coffee for us and bring it to the meeting room, and then when he was sitting down with his coffee, I pointed to what I had written in dry marker right across the top of the whiteboard:

DARRYL RIDLEY MANAGING DIRECTOR XYZ CARE LTD

Darryl did not see himself as the managing director, he didn't even see himself as the manager, but rather as an unwilling spare part forced into a position he had not asked for and did not want to be in, did not know enough about and so in reality he merely went through the motions of being in charge to fill his time on a daily basis.

My primary objective was to help Darryl see that he *could* be the manager in the real sense, because only at that point would he be able to assert himself over Amy and the other staff and only by doing that would the company have any hope at all of surviving after I had left at the end of my 6 month contract.

I shall never forget the look on Darryl's face as he read the words I had written on the white board. His face conveyed a mixture of shock, disbelief, and hope...all mixed up in the brief smirk that played across his face.

'Ok then Darryl, it's 2014, three years down the track, XYZ Care Ltd is now one of the major players in the region, you now have 5 offices throughout the county and you employ 100 staff.'

Darryl looked at me blankly. '5 offices? Huh, we can't even run the one we've got properly, never mind another four offices.' he moaned.

'Darryl, do me a favour, you've got some elastic bands out on Reception haven't you? Well would you pop along and get one for me please? Don't get a really big one, one this size will be perfect' I held my forefinger and thumb apart to signify the size I wanted.

Off he went and returned with a nice red elastic band of exactly the right size and handed it to me, with a quizzical look.

'Hold out your left hand please,' and as he did so I opened the band and putting his hand through it, left it on his wrist.

He asked what it was for and I told him I would tell him later, meanwhile we were going to concentrate on 2014, three years down the track.

'Darryl, close your eyes. Now imagine that this is your Head Office, imagine you've got 4 branches each with a manager and today is the day of your monthly management meeting here at Head Office. You are in early because you needed to prepare for the meeting because you have some good news to share as you've just signed a deal for another office and you want to float out that with 5 operations to run you'll be needing an Area Manager.'

Darryl looked up at me, 'But we can't even run this office, never mind five!'

'Darryl, hold out your left hand please!' My protégé dutifully held out his hand with a quizzical look on his face which soon turned to pain as I pinged the elastic band quite hard against the skin of his wrist.'

'Ouch! What did you do that for?' he scowled.

I then explained to Darryl that success comes in CANS and not CANT'S! I then gave him a mini seminar on the topic of mental default settings and mental governments, just exactly as you have learned earlier in this book! I explained all about the mental programming carried out unwittingly by ignorant but influential adults and that he was the product of the negative effect his mother had had on his self-belief, self-esteem and self-confidence through the comments she had thrown at him over the years...in fact Darryl was a 'text book' case of the potential of a perfectly capable child being destroyed by the negative comments of a domineering mother, totally ignorant of the damage she was doing to her son!

I quickly qualified my comments by explaining that many parents can be like this, not because they don't love their children, but because they just don't understand what they are doing when in moments of frustration they throw comments like, 'You clumsy idiot, can't you do anything right?'

Finally I explained that the words he used clearly indicated his default setting and the policies of his mental government in power, and that to help him become aware of the 'failure words' he habitually used that he was to listen carefully to his self-talk and the words he used and then, when he caught himself saying things like; 'Yeah but, I can't, I'll try (yes he got the Luke Skywalker story as well!) that he was to ping his wrist and in that way he would become very conscious of those words, and would then think before he uttered them and instead, think of what he CAN do and SHOULD do, rather than what he couldn't, wouldn't and shouldn't do!

Next, I set about working on Darryl's self-image because the fact is that nobody can perform at a level greater than the level at which they see themselves, i.e. their self- image. If Darryl saw himself as a scruffy and ineffective waste of space then that is precisely the level at which he would perform. My objective was to get him to be able to see himself as the Managing Director of the company!

After more than an hour of question, answer and explanation we got back to the whiteboard with DARRYL RIDLEY MANAGING DIRECTOR XYZ CARE LTD written in capitals at the top.

I asked Darryl to imagine that his managers had all arrived for the meeting, that they were laughing and chatting in a friendly manner as they made coffee outside the room. I asked him to look out of the window, I asked him to imagine their cars in the car park; a blue Peugeot 205, a silver Micra, a red Fiesta and a green Nissan Note. Then I asked him what kind of car was parked safely away in the corner of the car park.

'What do you mean? Do you mean my car?'

'Yes, exactly....your car, what kind would it be?'

Darryl thought for a moment and pulling the corners of his mouth down, replied,

'Dunno really, well, I suppose it would be a new Vauxhall Vectra like the one I've got now.'

'Really?' I replied....'You, the managing director of XYZ CARE LTD, a company with five offices and 100 staff, turning over a million a year? You would be driving a Vectra, would you? Are you sure about that?'

He smirked and told me he hadn't really thought about it, and so then for the next 20 minutes he got a mini seminar on the subject of vision and 'Imagination, a preview of your life's coming attractions!'

Following the mini seminar, I drew a line down the middle of the board and on the top left I wrote COMPANY and on the top right DARRYL.

Under 'COMPANY' I wrote FIVE SITES, under which came 100 EMPLOYEES, under which came £1,000,000,000 turnover, under which came £200,000 profit

Then I turned to the other side of the board and said to Darryl, 'Come on then Darryl , what would the managing director of a million pound company drive, what colour would it be, what colour would the seats be? We then chatted about his dream car list and finally settled on a Mercedes S 320.

'Why do I need to choose the colour now, what difference does it make?' he had asked.

Again I explained about the power of imagination and explained that I would soon be asking him to mentally sit in that car and if it had no colour it would have no form and if it had no form he couldn't get a picture of it to fix on the wall near his bed. Of course he had to have an explanation as to why he should have an image of a car next to his bed, and I told him it would all come together in while!

So at that point, under Darryl, as he had now decided on the colour, we wrote SILVER S 320 MERCEDES.

Then we talked about the kind of house he would live in, the powerboat he would like, the home cinema he would create in his house, the horses his wife would own...in fact once he started, I had trouble fitting it all on the board!

This was all about finding his 'Why' to do it; this was to be his reason, his motivation, his driver. I explained that the bigger the need, the bigger the motivation and the bigger the action required.

Next I took him to the staff room and made him stand in front of the mirror. I stood behind him, placed a hand on each shoulder and said, 'Darryl Ridley,

Managing director of XYZ Care Ltd, five branches, 100 staff and £1,000,000,000 annual turnover!'

I asked him to look at the person in the mirror and then asked him whether that person actually looked like the managing director of a large Care company? Jeans, trainers, sloppy sweatshirt, hair unkempt, stubble on his chin....a mess!

Then I asked him if the person in the mirror felt like the Managing Director of a large Care company. Darryl hung his head and replied 'No.'

I asked him if he really would like to become that managing director, and he agreed it would be a dream come true, which then led to a mini-seminar all about the principles of b-e-c-o-m-i-n-g the Managing Director, i.e.; that it would not be an overnight thing!

We returned to the meeting room and I explained that I was going to give him a complete makeover on the basis that to be the part he must think the part and look the part. I asked him if he had a suit to wear and he agreed that he had. I then asked him to imagine how he would feel walking down the street wearing that suit with a nice white shirt with cuff links, a tie with a nice splash of 'power dresser' red in it, a pair of highly polished black shoes, clean shaven, hair immaculate and carrying an equally shiny black briefcase to complete the image!

He agreed that he would look a million dollars dressed that way, that he could see that he would actually feel not only that he was something special, but also that he would feel confident and powerful within himself....

What came next, he was not at all prepared for!

I gave him a quick diagrammatic briefing on the whiteboard board about the Conscious Mind, the Subconscious Mind and the Solar Plexus, and how these all interact to connect with Universal Power to manifest into reality all the abundance that we desire. I spent a lot of time talking about the blindness of the Subconscious Mind and that it would accept without question everything that got fed down to it, especially the things fed down to it with highly charged positive or negative emotional energy.

I told Darryl about affirmations and how they helped manifest the abundance we wished for and gave him an affirmation that would help him b-e-c-o-m-e the person he wanted to become:-

'I am the managing director of the fastest growing Care Company in the region, I have fantastic staff. I am a savvy businessman and new opportunities to expand come to me through an ever increasing number of channels every month and I am so grateful for every good thing that keeps coming my way.'

As an aside, we have a range of proven affirmations to cover virtually every aspect of life and these are available simply be e-mailing us!

We worked on that one for a while until we had the kind of words he felt comfortable saying and believing. I told him to repeat that every day, during the day and every morning but most particularly every night before sleep.

I told him to get a picture of the exact Merc he wanted, to get a picture of a large group of women in size proportion to the Merc, and finally to get a picture of him in a suit, also in proportion to the Merc. Next I explained that as he was a bit of a computer geek he would have no difficulty scanning, cutting, copy and pasting in order to combine it all into ONE single picture of him standing next to the Merc as the MD, surrounded by this large group of women who would be his notional employees!

I explained that he would need to look at the picture every night before he went to bed, would need to get excited right down there in his solar plexus about having this as his reality and *believing* it because it is actually on its way! And then, when he was really excited to repeat his affirmation with a big heartfelt smile on his face!

I also told him that I wanted him to dress himself with his suit and briefcase once a week and stand in front of a full length mirror and repeat his affirmation out loud with a big smile on his face.

122

Next, having given him a 'check up from the neck up' complete with the 'prescription' he would need to take on a daily basis in order to become the MD, we spent the rest of the day on the key management and control system keys that would help him become a results orientated highly effective manager.

Finally, I explained that the business didn't need another passenger, that we needed more crew...and in particular we needed ...a Captain!

We discussed the business at some length and then agreed the key priorities and I explained that we must deal with the important and difficult FIRST and the least important last.

I explained the importance of having these priorities, or goals written down together with the dates/times they would be achieved. I agreed with him a complete week's work plan and key objectives that would fit into the 3 month horizon objective that we had agreed, so that he could have some distant perspective against which to measure our progress.

He would now no longer drift, now he would become a hungry goal seeking corporate killer!

His work day would begin at 08.30, he would come dressed as the MD and he would work through his priority list recording his results and we would meet the following Monday morning at 08.30am to review progress.

'But I live 80 miles away....I'll have to leave at 6.30am!'

I knew that if Darryl was to succeed he would have to change his slovenly attitude so I explained that people don't just 'slop' into success. This led to a brief extract from our 'Drum Tight and Razor Sharp' management seminar.

I explained that slack, dull edged people just don't succeed in life, and that neither would he unless he tightened up and sharpened up!

I turned to Darryl and with one of my most direct 'eye of the tiger' looks, I asked him if he wanted to be the MD or not, to which he replied, 'Yeah but....'

124

He never got a chance to finish the sentence before I grabbed his left arm and pinged the elastic band onto his wrist very hard and then, looking right into his eyes, I said in slow deliberate tones:- 'You *can* pay the price of success, or you *will* pay the price for failure. Your call, what's it going to be sunbeam?'

Before he could reply, I put my hand on his forehead and said in a very worried voice, 'Oh my God Darryl, I do believe you've got a bad case of HUB!'

'HUB, what's HUB?' he asked in surprise.

In serious tones I explained that it was disease that affected many in the 80% group, that it wasn't terminal and could actually be cured, however as long as he had the disease it would not be possible for him to succeed.

He looked at me with a flash of fear in his eyes and replied with a smile, 'Nah, you're joking, there's no such thing as HUB really is there?'

I replied, 'Yes there is and yes it's real and yes it will kill any chance of success before you even start, but I have the cure!'

'HUB stands for H, head, U, up, your B, butt, and as long as you've got your head up your but all you'll see is crap and crap are the results you'll get, so you'll give up.'

'This might be painful, but I'm going to rip your head right out of your butt once and for all so you *can* succeed, I owe it to your Ma!'

'Well I want to succeed of course.' He mumbled, to which I replied 'Well first thing to do is tell your face, because right now you look as if you already failed before you begin. If you want to succeed and have all the stuff on the board, you *must* do something about that default setting and get that useless government out of power so you can get Mr Rambo in and begin to get excited about your future, because without enthusiasm you ain't going to make it!

'Get on with it then Darryl, be very, very happy to start at 08.30, at 08.00, at 06.00 if need be and be happy to be able to pay the price from today....I STRONGLY suggest that you spend the rest of this day planning your work for the rest of the week based on the priorities we've discussed, with objectives set for each day. Then I STRONGLY suggest that you get up off your arse and get in here at 08.30 EVERY morning and you don't leave until you've achieved your goals for the day, even if it's 20.00 AND with your suit on and actually BE the managing director. Remember, your mother's business depends on it, any problems with that?'

I then explained that time was the only finite resource that Darryl possessed because his time on Earth had a finite start and would have a finite end...but that we didn't know when that would be, so best get the best from every minute!

To seal the deal I repeated Robert Smith's famous poem about the absolute value of time:-

The clock of life is wound but once,

> And no man has the power
>
> To tell just where the hands will stop
>
> At late or early hour.
>
> To lose one's wealth is sad indeed:
>
> To lose one's health is more:
>
> To lose one's soul is such a loss
>
> As no man can restore.
>
> The present only is our own,
>
> Live, Love, toil with a will --
>
> Place no faith in 'tomorrow' --
>
> For the clock may then be still.

Robert Hilton Smith July 21, 1928 - December 29, 2009

Following our session and the dawn of understanding, Darryl was finally awakening to opportunity and possibility and his determined look said it all as I bade him goodbye, reminding him that I would be back bright and early on Monday morning!

Well, the next Monday seemed to come round very quickly, and by 0845am we were sitting with coffee in the meeting room to go through Darryl's progress. Some things had been achieved, some had not. On those where he had succeeded he received gallons of praise, but when I began to dig into the other goals where he had not succeeded, it became obvious that once again he allowed himself to be side tracked by the distractions caused by other people and had once again also slipped back into NOT saying what NEEDED to be said because he didn't like to!

He was given an illustration of the potential results of the weak manager who shied away from doing the difficult things because they might upset 'Mary' and the results of the strong but pleasant manager whose priority was the business, and not to being a 'nice' pushover.

I explained that only by setting some objectives for staff to reach could they receive praise and recognition...something that babies cry for and soldiers die for!

I reinforced this by outlining the 'bully' manager who spent all his time trying to find people doing things wrong so he could ball them out for it and compared this with the 'leader' manager who got the team together, explained precisely what he wanted from them and set goals and then when he found them doing things right, heaped praise and recognition on the individuals concerned.

The employees of the weak manager and the bully manager bear no loyalty, arrive on the button and leave on the button, have little interest in their job and do it just for the money, whilst the 'colleagues' (change in term!) of the leader manager are prepared to go the extra mile because they are committed to the team and want to please the leader.

Employees resent the weak manager, hate the bully manager and would do anything for the leader manager and I finished up with this question; 'Which would you like to be?'

We will be covering effective management and team building skills in a later chapter.

I went on to explain that in a dynamic business like his, of course situations would arise to distract pre-set focus because situations would arise that could not be put to the back of the queue, things like staff sickness and the staff cover that would still be required to keep 'the show on the road,' however once these had been dealt with, he MUST return to the priority list again and stick at it until it was done.

I told him about the 'eye of the tiger', explaining that the tiger NEVER takes its eye from its prey from the moment of first seeing it to the moment it sinks its fangs in at the end, and that he must become the same if he wished to succeed.

Regrettably he gave me some excuses that resulted in him having to ping his wrist quite a bit, so that by the end of our session his wrist was becoming a bit red and sore...but it was working...he was learning!

Darryl had never had a mentor before to teach and help him. Certainly he had received plenty of scream sessions from his Ma about things that hadn't been done...but the charting of his success step by step along a planned 'climb,' he had never experienced before.

Several weeks later he had achieved a significant shift in his attitude such that he had actually given a member of staff a first and final written warning, something he had been too weak to do before.

This action raised his credibility in the eyes of the remainder of the staff and he now saw himself as the boss, his suit was his bosses' uniform and it helped him get respect. Towards Week 16 I began to let Darryl lead the meetings and I just acted as a sounding board for his proposals and by the time we had reached week 20 I knew he was going to succeed.

There, on the wall in his private office he had fixed a whiteboard with his targets for the next quarter written on it together with a 30 day action plan of who was going to do what and when to achieve it over those next 30 days, and best of all, considering he knew nothing about financial controls in the beginning, there he was sounding off to me about accounting matters using jargon like KPIs, and P&L!!

Darryl established himself during the next few months and I was subsequently pleased to hear from a Council Official that she had always seen him as a 'bit of a joke', but somehow he was different now and she was very pleased to note that when they carried out their last inspection, instead of noting down reams of 'Still Outstanding From Previous Inspection,' things were getting done, and he was making strong progress towards being one of the best Care companies in the region!

Perhaps as you look ahead you will realise and accept that like Darryl, the only person standing between where you are now and the success and abundance you are searching for and are totally capable of achieving ....is YOU!

An elastic band is a very cheap investment, but it certainly does work if you want to create a new habit; however it takes 30 days to create a new habit. Habits are formed by consistent actions and each time the action is performed a silken thread is formed, over weeks of repetition that thread becomes as thick as string, then as thick as rope as even more time passes, until ultimately it becomes as thick as a steel hawser. Now you've got a new habit!

However, understand this; once you start, all you need is one slip back that needs a 'ping'....and you have to go back to Day I and start your 30 days all over again!

If you utilise the information contained in this session, it will certainly help you dramatically improve your performance either in your management career or your own business and most certainly you will begin to get noticed by your boss as the new high flyer whose highly efficient competence has begun to outshine the competition and place him or her streets ahead!

Incidentally, we know that it is only possible to make one first impression and if the one you made was not as good as it could be, don't worry, if you persist in developing yourself and consistently turn in great performance, that *will* be noticed and recognised!

CHAPTER 7

MANAGER TYPES

The definition of management right at the start of this book caused us to begin with *you* because we learned from the definition that the most difficult entity to manage is one's 'self'.

Hopefully you found enough content and information to at least open the door to how you tick and how to improve your 'self' so that it becomes a highly effective device for helping you achieve all your goals, so now we are going to investigate management!

We will begin by reminding ourselves of the definition we read at the start:

Management in all business and organizational activities is the act of coordinating the efforts of people to accomplish desired goals and objectives using available resources efficiently and effectively. Management comprises planning, organising, staffing, leading, directing, and controlling an organisation (a group of one or more people or entities) or effort for the purpose of accomplishing a goal.

Resourcing encompasses the deployment and manipulation of human resources, financial resources, technological resources, and natural resources.

Let's focus on the first sentence. Here we read that there are two elements; people and resources,

Controlling resources is perhaps the easiest aspect of management, on the other hand I'm sure we have seen many examples of highly intelligent, narrow focus 'bean counters' who are great at balancing the books but are absolutely crap at achieving results as Business Managers!

Why?

Because whilst they can understand what the numbers are telling them they should do, unless they are a one man band, they must do those things through people and it is here that this group crash and burn every time, because people skills and team building are just *not* their forte, although they could learn!

So, we will focus on the people dynamic first.

We alluded to some of the 'people management' issues encountered by poor old Darryl in the previous chapter and now we are going to get down to business and review those management types.

First of all we must understand that there is a very significant difference between being a manager and being a leader and we could simplistically say that managers manage, but leaders lead as well as manage.

So what is the difference?

The 'Manager' manager

On his appointment a manager is given the limits of his authority and the parameters within which he must operate.

Think of it this way; the manager must operate within the specific circle of power that has been accorded to him by the delegation of authority in order to carry out

138

his responsibilities and produce the results he is tasked to produce.

Everyone is familiar with retail stores, so as our example let's put the sales floor manager into the spotlight. Let's suppose that his circle of power includes the security staff on the entrance doors, the customer service desk, the checkouts and the shop floor staff who must keep all the shelves full.

In order to effectively manage his department, he must primarily interact with the cash office and the stockroom. The former to ensure that tills are cleared regularly and that they always have sufficient change of the various denominations required to keep things running smoothly, and the latter to ensure that there is always an adequate and timely delivery of stock to the sales-floor when requested by sales floor staff.

The cash office and stockroom are not within the manager's circle of power, yet without their cooperation his department would begin to suffer and then this would impact on store sales performance.

All business operations, once trading, settle down to operate at what we might refer to as a 'performance norm'.

That is to say that the 'newness' has worn off and whilst those involved may have really pulled out all the stops at the start and produced excellent performance, now their performance level has sunk to just above acceptable, so that they do enough to be 'OK' and sufficient to stay out of trouble, they no longer push themselves to achieve 'best possible' as they did in the beginning.

In other words they are now 'average' and our definition of average is; 'best of the worst, the worst of the best...the cream of the crap.'

Who wants to be average?!

So our manager and his department are now operating at 'average ok'...however, given that this scenario will not just apply to his department in isolation, it will in all probability also apply to the stockroom personnel as well, which in turn will reflect in the rate of stock replenishment, which in turn will reflect on availability of products and in turn the quality of the sales floor displays, which in turn will of course reflect on the level of achievable sales...which are average!

'Manager' managers tend not to mould their staff into an effective team, which can only be achieved through a gradual process that requires specific skills on the manager's part and the introduction of certain dynamics. To achieve this it is essential to hold regular team meetings, something that 'manager' managers do not do in the true sense and meaning of the term 'team meetings', however they may possibly have their staff together from time to time to pass on information and hand out demotivating bollockings, which is not quite the same thing as we shall see later when we discuss the leader manager.

'Leader' manager

Whereas the 'manager' manager only has his own circle of power through which to get results, the leader manager also develops circles of influence as well.

What do we mean by circles of influence?

Those employees within a 'manager' manager's circle of power are in his control and must do what he says they must do, not necessarily because they want to, but because they *have* to...ultimately their job depends on it! The downside of course is that the 'manager' manager can only influence those within his circle of power *and has no influence over people or events outside his circle of power.*

In contrast the leader manager is able not only to control those within his circle of power, but is also able to *influence* those *outside* his circle of power but *inside* his circle of influence. Due to this, he has the potential to achieve far higher levels of success than the 'manager' manager simply because he is able to not only call upon those within his circle of power, but also those outside it, where he or she has influence.

A point to bear in mind; those who are in the leader manager's circle of influence do not have to do anything he or she asks of them because they are not within the leader manager's circle of power...but they do things for the leader manager because they *want* to!

This is one of the facets that drive the leader manager to far higher levels of success than the 'manager' manager can possibly aspire to, simply because he or she is able to *leverage* the level of influence they have over others, whereas the 'manager' manager cannot.

How do we transit from being a 'manager' manager into being a Leader manager and enjoy improved performance?

Do you have to run around smiling like an idiot, singing and shedding sweetness and light over a cynical group of employees?

No, of course not, but there are ways in which the Manager manager can *develop* those skills and it would be best to begin by accepting the notion that you *cannot* be a leader without a team, so let's begin with team building!

I love that moment in the film 101 Dalmations where a group of dogs goes charging past the camera, followed a few moments later by a single dog who howls, 'I'm the leader, which way did they go?'

It's not possible to lead from behind and that particular doggy was certainly *not* the leader because the leader was the doggy that was out in front *leading* the pack!

Once more perhaps it's best to illustrate how the leader manager operates by once more telling a real live story...this time it's Nancy's story!

CHAPTER 8

FROM No 67 to No 1

The background is a national retail group struggling during a recession, where morale and disgruntlement reigned supreme. Staff turnover amongst the management group was high and those that stayed, stayed only because at the time in question there were few jobs and little opportunity.

The attitude of the company toward the management group at that time was, 'If you can't hack it we can soon find 10 people who will.'

A very uplifting and inspirational way of getting peak performance, Nancy will continue the story!

I took over an area of 21 stores and at the time I took it over, the area was cumulatively 67th out of 71 areas within the company performance league table.

This league table evaluated and factored in all the KPI's and churned out a whole list of data expressed across

145

the top of a spread sheet and each area's performance in each sector working left to right and in the final column on the right came the overall score followed by the area's position.

67th out of 71 and running at a loss!

A pretty dire situation and when I looked at all the serious shortfalls indicated by the KPIs, I knew that I had a monumental task on my hands if the area was to be raised from dismal malaise into vibrant life!

My predecessor had left for her own reasons, but judging by the results she left behind it was clear she had not been coping for quite a while and the stress must have been enormous.

I had already been through the financials so I decided that my first objective should be to introduce myself to the people in the stores. In fact introducing myself was not my objective at all, what I wanted was to get an indication of the 'government in power' of the key

146

personnel in each store and I would be able to gain this by listening carefully to the words they used and the situations they discussed.

Evaluating the people was in fact far more important than evaluating the store because the store will always be a reflection of the Manager, and the Manager will operate at his or her default setting and in turn their government in power, which is more difficult to change than the physical layout of the store.

So it was almost a week filled with coffee, body language watching, monitoring eye contact or lack of it and keen listening and sensing and wearing my best smile!

I made it my business to introduce myself and talk to everyone I walked past during my time at each store and to really 'feel' it! What I mean by that is to detect the dominant vibrations which are powerful keys in identifying undercurrents and the personality types of those who worked there.

It's quite amazing what you can divine about what goes on behind the scenes if you are sensitive to undercurrents!

Some stores vibrated at happy and positive, others at miserable and negative. Just as I am able to detect these vibrations so are customers and the more happy, positive the vibrations the more comfortable the shopping experience becomes and the longer the customer will stay and the more he or she will make that store their destination of choice when other competitor options are available, so vibrations are very important as they affect turnover!

As well as evaluating people, I was asking a lot of questions about the problems they faced, the issues that they considered were holding them back or making life difficult for them.

Since I already knew the key issues of each store from the financials I had been studying, I had a fair idea what I was about to find as I walked in the store and it was

148

matters relating to these things that I left a job list for the manager to complete within 7 days.

Whilst I may have noted maybe up to 70 items that required attention, I issued a maximum of only 20 for initial completion simply because it is so easy for a manager to become overwhelmed, so little and often is far more effective than a massive dollop every now and then!

Once out in the car I wrote a brief summary of my perception of the vibration of the store and the manager and his or her attitudes. I evaluated the body language I had seen, the words and word clusters people had used, the physical condition of the store and from all of this I was able to determine the manager's default setting and government in power.

From my financial evaluation and my brief tour of the sales area and stockrooms, I was able to set up a key-area action plan, for not only improving the store, but also for improving the manager of the store. I gave each manager a score out of 10 and each store a score out of 10.

I realised that my immediate priority was to attend to the stores where standards and results were unacceptable and so my second visit was concentrated on these managers. The first thing I did was to open my file containing the key-area action list and check the things that had been completed.

Some managers had completed all the tasks set for them, however others had not and where there was a shortfall, I asked for the reasons why.

Where some were acceptable, staff sickness or delivery failure for example, others, where the excuse had been, 'I just haven't got round to it' were not. This was just not acceptable.

Remember that each excuse is very likely to be a thin shell of truth stuffed with a lie, so don't accept anything that does not vibrate at 100% genuine!

Now it is at this point that nice Nancy becomes the not so nice Nancy, where the beaming smile is replaced with a face that would frighten even Rosa Klebb, the Russian lady spymaster in the James Bond films, whilst her beautiful dancing blue eyes become cold as ice as they bore laser like through to the back of the unfortunate individual's skull as the excuses are ripped to shreds!

This is not an experience that the individual is likely to want to repeat and so the key action list is reset with some new objectives and the individual is told that these must all be completed by a specific day. Now all of a sudden there is a sense of urgency and focus and a change from the lethargic to the almost frenetic!

Just as I had finished my first set of visits, a crop of stock-results came in from Head Office. For those readers who are not familiar with the term 'stock result,' this is when the Stock-Take team visits a store, count all the stock and calculate a value. This is then transmitted to Head Office who analyse bankings and then calculate the physical sum of money that has been lost during the 6 monthly or yearly period.

If the cash loss equated to more than a certain pre-set percentage of turnover, an investigation had to be launched as these cash losses were straight off the bottom line. Losses could originate from a variety of sources; theft of stock by customers, theft of stock and cash by staff, failure to get credit for returns to suppliers and short deliveries not claimed for, to name but a few!

This crop of results revealed some serious issues in several stores which led me to carry out forensic investigations to establish the cause of the losses.

In all of the cases I investigated, serious lack of control and management incompetence were significant causal factors.

Once my investigations were complete I held meetings with the managers concerned and highlighted the causes of the losses and made sure that when the finger of blame was pointed elsewhere they knew that 3 other fingers were pointing at them.

Due to the seriousness of what I had found, I was obliged to issue 'first and final' written warnings to some managers, this reverberated throughout the Area leaving nobody in any doubt that I meant business!

This was followed by a session that I call 'the invitation to step over the line.'

Basically, during this session I outline the vision I hold for the area and invite them to step over the line and join me...or take the alternative which will ultimately lead to dismissal having gone through the due process.

During these sessions I have noted a range of emotions from tears to sullen resistance.

During this process I made decisions about who was at risk of not making the transition from the manager in name and cross the line and become the manager in actuality, and so I set up interviews for managers

153

designate to be employed and trained by managers in the training stores I had created ready to fill any potential gaps if the flaky individuals did not make it.

After 6 weeks I held my first management meeting which was a significant step in the process of welding all these individuals into the highly motivated team I wanted to create. It was the first they had ever attended!

What had amazed me since taking on the Area, was that few of the managers actually knew each other and it is obvious a team can't be built out of individuals who don't know each other.

One of the stores had a large first floor room that was disused and I had decided to convert this into a training room. I had the room re-decorated and I bought tables and chairs from a local second hand shop as I had no budget set aside for this expense. I also wanted to create a totally positive environment and so I purchased a large selection of positive message posters with which to decorate the walls and create the atmosphere I wanted.

I had a very large polystyrene cut out of the Area's designation, A43, and had this fixed on the far wall together with the slogan 'A43 Rocks!'

This was to be the management group's first encounter with what I wanted to create, and I can still see the faces of the delegates as they came in and took in the atmosphere, theme and style of the room!

One of the first things I hit was gossip! I told them that I would not tolerate gossip, whinging, moaning or negative comment about other team members, the Company, Head Office or anything else for that matter in any way shape or form. This set the stage for the ethos I wanted to cultivate within the Area.

It was here that I planned to share the vision, that A43 was going to be Number 1 within 12 months, that the entire group was going to attend the twice yearly corporate event where attendance was not mandatory, that I would provide a coach to take everyone including me to the venue, that some managers in the Area were going to win prizes!

It was in this meeting that the very first group training session that any of these Managers had ever attended was delivered. I also used the session to focus on the key results that we, as a team, would need to achieve during the next 4 weeks and that my prime function would be to monitor results and unblock any blockages outside store control that might be causing issues.

I have always agreed with the Japanese management principle that sees the management group as the server of the 'worker' group where their mission is to make sure the 'worker group' has everything it needs to enable them to produce the highest possible quality of output. This is in contrast to the British hierarchical model where top management tend to keep themselves away from the 'shop floor' and its problems!

Just a point of clarification here; I am not advocating that you as the manager leave the bridge of your ship to work in the engine room, simply because if you did, who would be up there steering and making sure the ship was going in the right direction? That does not mean however that you should not sometimes roll your sleeves up, get stuck in and work alongside your staff. It helps to show them that you are a team member just like them, and of course that you are all in it together!

Remember the circle of power and the circle of influence?

I, as an Area Manager had power over all my staff, however in order to achieve the outstanding results I wanted to achieve, I realised that I would have to develop a wide a circle of influence as well!

I began to talk to Company Reps and explain what we were striving to achieve and gained their help in getting us improved product supply, more convenient delivery times and prizes that could be awarded to members of staff who achieved the best sales of their focus products.

Clearly Head Office executives held a lot of power and I realised that if I could develop some allies there, that they could be enormously helpful in sorting out any problems the Area faced. I made it my business to meet these people when I was at Head Office and also I was not afraid to put a call through to ask for their help in solving issues that were impacting negatively on the Area's performance and which were outside my control

I have always operated the principle of the 'Love Bank Account', although in a commercial context 'love' is perhaps not the right word to use and 'credit' may be more appropriate.

This process involves putting in 'credits' or favours into the Love Bank Account of individuals that I hoped to bring into my circle of influence. In explanation, let's suppose that I had asked for the help of a HO executive to sort out a problem for me. Once the action had been taken and the result achieved I would send an e-mail or sometimes, if it was a big thing, a hand written card to tell them the benefit that their help had brought and to thank them personally for their intervention.

Later, when I began to produce an Area News Letter I made sure their names appeared as it was also circulated to the 'top brass.'

In this way I gradually extended my circle of influence which then increased my leverage and ability to get results.

During the weeks that followed that first meeting, I would visit stores and check progress towards objectives and either praise or push, depending on what I found.

Let me introduce a powerful development concept here; always look to find people doing things 'right', rather than constantly look for what people are doing 'wrong'.

To be able to do this you must first explain exactly what you want, how you want it to be done and if appropriate, give a quantified target of the result you expect. This enabled me to visit stores looking for what people were doing right and then when I found it, I could take that member of staff and praise them publicly for what they had achieved, call other members of staff over to show them what 'Mary' had done, holding her work and standards up as an example of what I wanted.

Based on that little adage about recognition; 'Babies cry for it, soldiers die for it,' I have proved time and time again that praising what you want more of is a far more effective success tool that kicking what you don't want. People love recognition and they love praise and as the adage suggests, people will do a great deal to get another sincere 'Well done!' and a pat on the back.

On the point of dishing out praise, always make sure you have direct eye contact with the individual as you say the words and remember that even greater value can be added by putting your hand on their shoulder or upper arm as you say the words of praise...with a big smile of course!

Most Managers have been brought up to find people doing things wrong and kicking them for it, as I have explained however, my philosophy is the opposite and because of this, as the weeks passed and I went round my stores, it was like watching a flower gradually opening into bloom!

At my next management meeting I was able to do some other things that had never been done before!

I dished out prizes to those who had attained the target set the previous month. I called them to the front and led the applause myself. As well as this, if it was appropriate, I sometimes invited the National Account Manager of a manufacturing company in to make a short speech about their company and hand out prizes for sales of their product, all which made the presentation even more special. As well as this, I sometimes invited a Head Office executive to speak and on some occasions even got a management trainer in. All of this made attending team meetings something to look forward to, rather than the arse kicking norm that some Managers call team meetings!

From this you will begin to appreciate how the general level of motivation within the Area was gradually and steadily raised. How this group of disparate individuals became welded into a highly effective and highly motivated team and how, in doing so, I was able to extend my circle of influence even further by involving those from outside my circle of power.

When the time came for the next twice annual Head Office session, A43 fielded a full team on the coach that took us there, an unheard of situation, and guess what? Several Managers did win prizes and of course I was there with a camera to record the happy event for the next newsletter. At the end we all formed up for a group photograph which eventually finished up as the front of a Christmas card we created to send to all Head Office personnel...more expansion of the circle of influence!

Our objective was to become No1 Area in the company within a year.

A43 went from No67 out of 72, to No1 in just 7 months and the pride this produced within the team was such that if we had asked them to give up a week of their holiday and work, they would gladly have done so.

CHAPTER 9

THE PERSONAL 'CREDIT' ACCOUNT

We have just gone through many months of concentrated effort explained by Nancy in a single chapter, and so we think it would be of benefit if we looked at the key issues that were in play during those months that A43 went from the bottom and up to No 1.

We read somewhere a long time ago that the leader will get the results the leader has the right to expect.

Quite an interesting statement if you take the bones out of it; getting the results you have the right to expect.

This brings us back to another point; there is no such thing as weak leadership simply because it is not possible to lead weakly. The word leadership is about passion, dynamism, strength, conviction and charisma. Sorry, but weak people cannot possibly have those qualities, however they *could* develop them!

So...the leader *will* get the results he or she has the right (deserves) to expect because leaders are people who are dynamic, strong, filled with conviction and exude charisma because of the passion and enthusiasm they have for their vision.

We established earlier that in order to be a leader, one must have **vision**.

If a leader (an individual with followers) is to achieve an objective then the leader must share the vision with passionate conviction in order to inspire the followers. I love the film Spartacus, here a slave goes on to lead an army of slaves against the might of the Roman army. This really proves that leadership does *not* come with rank, so don't think for a moment that just because your name badge carries the word 'Manager' that the badge makes you a leader and that people will follow you. No, all that means is that you have a circle of power in which others must obey your reasonable instructions, a very different thing!

Ok, so now we have a crystal clear defined image of the vision we hold, what next?

The vision must now be **manifested** into reality. So let's suppose that you are the Manager of a large retail store and that ever since you took over from the previous Manager, you have never liked the way the departments are laid out on the sales floor. You just know that if you changed things round so that the high demand staple items, sugar for example, were located at the back of the store rather than at the front, then in order to get to the sugar customers would be exposed to promotions and offers as they walked to the back of the store and that because of this, your sales would increase.

Next issue; people hate change! We know that some of the regular customers might be a little annoyed until they get used to the change, but we also know that the sales floor staff who will have to physically make the changes won't like it either because of all the extra work that will be involved.

The leader must share the vision in a highly positive and enthusiastic way with the team, fully promoting all the benefits that increased turnover will bring to the store, which in turn will result in improved bonus benefits for the team once the changes are made and the expected turnover increases begin to flow through the checkouts.

In order to manifest the change into reality we must plan. Important point here! Always involve others in the planning stage, nobody wants change *imposed* upon them. It is only through consultation and the gaining of views and ideas from the team that they can begin to feel *ownership*. Once they do they will work far harder and to a far higher standard than if it's a case of at the team briefing, 'Right guys, this is what we're going to do and we'll start next Monday at 6pm after the store has closed.'

It is essential to include some of the team's ideas *where possible*, however since your team is not a democracy, yours must be the final decision!

Interesting point; a man who visited a vast building site asked one of the men who was laying bricks what he was building and the man told him, 'a wall.' Further on he asked another man what he was doing and he looked up above the level that he had built and replied, 'I'm helping build a beautiful cathedral.'

Perhaps the guy in charge of the first man was a manager, whilst the guy in charge of the second man was a leader who conveyed a vision!

I wonder which man built to the higher standard?

If you have vision but do nothing to execute that vision into reality, then you might as well be building castles in the sky!

The second man was **inspired** by his boss and throughout history, right up to this day, we see time after time that the difference between achieving *outstanding* results as opposed to *mediocre* results hinges on the passion and inspiration of a leader who has a firm conviction that his or her vision can be made into reality and shares this with total passion and enthusiasm with the team.

Something to bear in mind at this point. The passion and inspiration the leader shares with his team, is a little like deodorant...we can't just apply it once and expect to smell nice ever after! Equally, if the dream is to be kept alive in your team then the passion and inspiration they feel must be applied constantly, just like deodorant, until the vision becomes reality.

People often tell us that they can't be charismatic because they weren't born charismatic. This is simply not true. Charisma is exuded when someone is utterly obsessed with their vision and shares that vision with a passion that sweeps others before it and attracts them to be part of it like a powerful magnet can attract nails!

We have already said that there can be no such thing as weak leadership since each word is basically a contradiction of the other, a little like saying, 'hot ice cube!' Leaders must exude power and **drive** if they are to attract others to the cause and keep them focussed.

When I was a child, some small toy cars were fitted with a friction drive motor. This was basically a flywheel attached to the two drive wheels at the back of the car. To make it shoot over the carpet I had to push it hard along the carpet for about a foot and quickly repeat the process several times until the little motor was screaming it's little head off, then the little car was released and it would shoot away, gradually slowing down, until the motor ran out of power and finally stopped.

We can use this as an analogy to show the drive required to keep the show on the road, the drive required to keep the mission focussed, and the drive required to maintain effort *despite what might happen to affect the plan,* so that in the end, the vision can become the reality.

If you don't keep revving up your team then like my little friction drive car, then it will gradually run out of energy, and stop!

Of course to keep the team focussed the leader must remain focussed. The leader cannot allow the trivial or the fairly irrelevant to distract him or her long from the mission in hand, equally the leader knows that obstacles in the path are there to be overcome.

What happen if things go wrong? People who blame others for situations that affect them are in reality allowing themselves to be victims of 'someone else' simply because, by their own admission, that 'someone else' has obviously got the power to affect them…because they did.

We always take 100% responsibility and the **ownership** of everything that happens to us and so we are never victims of 'someone else'. We are totally responsible for us, and in fact Nancy came up with a winner a couple of years ago when she said, 'We are the conclusion of all our decisions.'

Great line isn't it? How awful it would be to say instead, 'We are the conclusions of all of someone else's decisions.' That would mean we are the slaves of others, to do with us as they wish...a condition that is complete anathema to us!

Failing to take responsibility indicates a weakness in an individual's character and is a roadblock to success which is why the Sales Rep who blames his product, his area, his boss, his support staff, the strength of the competition, can never succeed. All of those excuses are *external* factors and it is not *until* he or she verbalises and *internalises* that 'if it's to be it's up to *me!*' And, 'I am responsible for me,' can success possibly be achieved.

Never ever utter the loser's mantra, 'It's not my fault.'

When Nancy took over A43 she realised (obviously) that it was staffed by *people*!

Why make this point? The leader can never hope to lead his or her team effectively unless they realise that their team members have a life that extends *outside* work and the degree of happiness they enjoy outside work will have an impact on their performance in work.

Stop! No, we are not going to suggest that the leader must become some kind of corporate agony aunt!

No, what we a*re* going to suggest is that without prying, the leader invests a small amount of time casually finding out about the lives of key players in the team.

This will help in several ways. If you don't know that Susan has a 19 year old son called Sam who is at Uni on a Business Management degree, how can you ask how he's getting on?

The answer is of course you can't!

Why is this important? We have a concept called the 'Love Bank' for family and friends remember, but we change it to a 'Credit Bank' for corporate environments!

Let us explain how it works. For example, you take just 3 minutes in passing to ask Susan how young Sam is getting on and then you give her a moment to tell her about when you were at Uni...That is a credit deposit made into the You-Susan Credit Account, but not only that, because of this *and* your genuine smile, you are being *charismatic*.

Susan thinks you are a wonderful, caring boss because you take an interest in her and the other members of the team. You constantly look to find people doing things *right* and recognising them for it rather than doing things *wrong* and criticising them for it.

You can make big deposits when it's a subordinate's birthday by organising a drink after work for example, or at Christmas by making sure the team all go out together for a bit of a party.

As time goes by those credits continue to click up as you drop in yet more and more in passing. Ultimately, the time will come when you want Susan to do something

174

for you that will perhaps mean working a bit extra. As there is a nice lump of positive credit in your account with her, she will more than likely be delighted to help you.

This is one of the keys to building a harmonious and happy hard working team.

Imagine the opposite! The manager who never smiles, is always on their case, where nothing is ever good enough, who is always looking for what is wrong and ignoring what is right.

The manager who knows *nothing* of the personal circumstances of his people and sees them merely as work units, resources to be used. If *he* asked Susan to stay late to help him, the answer would probably be no!

Suppose, for example, that Jill is a line manager of yours. Jill's performance has been slipping a little lately. You know she has a troublesome teenage daughter, so when you ask Jill to come and have a coffee in the office, you can raise the matter of your concern about her performance which until a month ago was always outstanding. You then ask if everything is OK at home, she then tells you her daughter, Mandy, is being a bit of a worry.

You can't do anything to help her directly, but by *empathising* with her she knows that you care, which of course also adds to the credit bank.

Notice we said *empathise* and not *sympathise*.

As an analogy consider this; empathy is when someone is in a hole and you throw them a rope and help them out...sympathy is where you jump into the hole with them and hold a 'pity party,' so you can never help them out!

Empathise because empathy focuses on the solution. *Never* sympathise because sympathy focuses on the problem and because of this, sympathy is negative as it does nothing to help people overcome the challenge they face.

CHAPTER 10

ASSERTION

As we pointed out at the beginning of this book, as you progress across the vast plains of your career in management you will inevitably encounter the lions who will want to kill you, the hyenas who will want to take a lump out of you when you're looking the other way, and of course the other gnus who will nip you if they can!

To give human form to these denizens of the plains, the lions are the bully bosses whose sole aim is to continually find fault in all you do and then mentally abuse you for it. Next the hyenas, they are your colleagues who may be jealous of you or plain and simple nasty people who will stitch you up at every opportunity. Finally we have the gnus, they are your staff and amongst them you may find some resentful subordinates, these are the ones who will try to railroad your plans and often try to make you look silly from a safe distance.

Of course amongst all of this aggression, we also have the doves who may be at any level in the management structure. These are the people who take an interest in you and want to help you succeed in any way they can.

From this analogy we see that we need a methodology for taking on the lions and the hyenas which is a separate methodology from taking on the gnus.

Let's deal with the lions and hyenas first.

When another person constantly abuses their power over us and we find them utterly unreasonable, then our aim must be to send a very clear message that will change the way that individual habitually interacts with us, so they are no longer abusive.

Clearly, when we reach the decision to deal with the matter, it will not have been in response to a 'one off' situation, but a whole catalogue of events over a period of time. Since this is so, we have the opportunity to take some time and 'design' our message and not 'shoot from the hip,' which is always a dangerous thing to do!

We must carefully craft our message in such a way that it does not cause the individual to defend him or herself excessively.

Let's suppose that our Manager, Bill, constantly rubbishes most of the contributions we offer at management meetings. These put downs can include Bill catching the eye of another person and rolling his eyes whilst you are talking, to looking down at the table whilst you are speaking, to outright verbal hostility.

This behaviour makes you dread management meetings and because of the way you have been treated you have now grown reluctant to offer any contribution.

What we must do with Bill is to arrange a private meeting to discuss some areas of concern that you have.

Once you attend the meeting and Bill asks you what it's all about, you can deliver Part One of the Three-Part Assertion Message.

First we need to specify the **behaviour** that we want Bill to change, and so we might say something like this; 'Bill, when we hold our management meetings and I offer a contribution and you just dismiss it out of hand...

Next we need to explain our **feelings** about being treated in this way.

... I feel you do not value me as a Manager and a worthwhile member of your team and because of this...

Then we need to convey the **effect** this treatment has upon us as a Manager

...I just don't feel that I want to make any more contributions to the challenges our team faces, and because of this I no longer feel a worthwhile member of the team.

Picking up on the three key areas:

Behaviour: The behaviour we would like to see changed must be described very accurately and objectively, or Bill may not clearly understand what behaviour you find offensive.

You must ensure that Bill understands very clearly that his behaviour diminishes your self-esteem.

You must be very specific and not vague about how you describe Bill's conduct.

Never include any comments about Bill's motives, attitudes or character, as this *will* cause Bill to defend himself.

Make your description of Bill's behaviour an objective statement rather than a judgment, also avoid terms like never, always, and constantly. Avoid profanity at all costs.

When you disclose your feelings, convey precisely how you feel about the effect Bill has on you during the management meeting.

The inclusion of emotion into your statements (please don't cry!) underscores just how important the assertion is for you.

Never use judgemental words as these *will* create the need for Bill to defend himself, which is not our objective.

In terms of describing the effect of Bill's treatment upon you, a short concise message that cites a concrete and tangible effect that you experience will normally encourage Bill to change his behaviour and meet your needs.

Let's take another example.

Suppose Bill is a hard man manager and talks in a harsh and aggressive tone

183

Behaviour; 'When you speak to me so angrily...'

Feelings; 'I feel embarrassed and disrespected, and as a result I feel that I'm completely useless...'

Effects: 'And I try to avoid meeting with you, especially when other people are around.'

Nobody should have to work with an abusive boss and the fact is that this individual will keep behaving in that way until they are pulled up about it. The two examples of how to deal with an abusive lion work very well and whatever the situation, couch your conversation into; behaviour, feelings and effect.

So how do we deal with the hyenas? Exactly the same! These are colleagues, or people on the same level as you and the reason for the way they treat you with disrespect could possibly be to score points in front of the boss, or because they are jealous of you and they are trying to demean you.

What about gnus who try to nibble at you?

Frequently these are long serving people who have been passed up for promotion, have seen it all before and resent you, the young manager being in charge.

These types of people can, if treated properly, be a tremendous asset, but equally they can be as stubborn as a mule and a thorn in your side.

Let's take some examples.

You have been appointed manager of a department that Jerry has been working in for 16 years. He is 52 and you are 25. Jerry applied for promotion several times during the early years of his employment but was always turned down. During those 16 years he has seen them come and he has seen them go, so when you started he went round the other gnus saying things like, 'Got another new wonder boy/girl to train! Do you know what I was asked to do today? Ridiculous, they all come with these big ideas...'

Jerry is not your friend and he will do all he can to undermine you. He may even deliberately drop you right in it if he can get away with it, perhaps by deliberately not telling you something that if you had known, would have stopped you taking a certain course of action.

You can either tolerate Jerry's behaviour or deal with it. Let's hope you decide to deal with it!

The best way to operate when you take on your new appointment is to watch very carefully what goes on with the people who work within your circle of power. Listen carefully to who says what to whom. Then, having observed behaviour, decide who the leader is. That is the person you need to get on your side and once you do that you will find that the others will automatically follow like sheep…(gnus??)

If, despite your best efforts they stubbornly refuse to join you, then unfortunately its 1,2,3 and down the road using the company's disciplinary procedure.

So, let's suppose you've been paying attention to the gnus as they go about their daily tasks and you have decided that good old long serving Jerry is the leader, the only issue is that he is negative and is always against every new thing you try to introduce to make things better and more efficient.

How do you deal with Jerry?

First make a list of both positive and negative aspects of Jerry's actual performance on the job and then carefully plan what you will be saying to Jerry to get him to 'cross the line' and join you...or otherwise!

Once that has been done, choose your moment carefully and invite Jerry in for a 'chat' on the pretext that you want to get his views on something.

This theme, where you treat Jerry as someone very experienced with a valuable opinion to give, is one that needs to flow through the whole meeting.

In outline, the way this could go is something like this; 'Jerry, I want to pick your brains about xyz, so let's grab a coffee in the office.'

Jerry now thinks that his unofficial status as leader has been recognised by you, so he will not suspect your real motive!

As you sit down, make sure that there are no physical barriers between the two of you and also that there will be no interruptions. Maybe you sit at the desk (position of power) whilst you invite him to sit alongside you so he can see some documents on the desk. If you are right handed, sit him on your left and vice versa if you are left handed.

Now the scene is set and armed with a coffee, you can now discuss this new development and hear his views.

Jerry will have much to say, possibly all negative and if this is the case, then the best response is; 'Yes, I know how you feel, when the Area Manager first told me

188

about it I felt the same way as you, but then when I thought about it some more, I began to see there will be some real benefits, bla bla for example.'

Nodding your head and with a smile continue with, 'Does that make sense?'

Body language is an amazing thing and when you nod your head with a genuine smile and say those words people are more inclined to duplicate your body language and agree.

If, as the discussion flows, Jerry agrees with you about the positives then you are home and dry. If he doesn't agree, then your fall-back is, 'Ok then. I take your point, but the plain fact is we have no choice. It must be done, so let's discuss how best to do it.'

That response works better than 'Tough shit, it's going to be done and that's all there is to it.'

Once that part of the discussion is over, you need to move to stage two of your plan. By this time Jerry will

189

be a little more malleable than if you had gone in cold on the negatives you really invited him in to discuss.

Who is the most important person to Jerry? Why Jerry of course, so the next thing to do is get him to start talking about his favourite subject; Jerry.

Ask open ended questions, the ones that cannot be answered with a straight yes or no, and in that way you will be able to achieve that open communication which is vital if you want your message to reach the target *and* be accepted by Jerry.

'Bet you've seen a lot of changes in your time Jerry, what has been the biggest change yet?'

Master the art of silence! Silence is a very important part of effective communication. People hate silence and because they feel so uncomfortable with it they feel obliged to fill it with words, so if you wait long enough, *they* will inevitably break the silence.

No, it's not some Kung Fu process, it just means that once you have asked the question and remain silent, and then the other person always feels compelled to fill the silence.

Wait with raised eyebrows and a smile and the answer will eventually come.

Once you've got a dialogue running you can open it out by probing his personal life.

'Your kids are both married now aren't they Jerry, got any grandchildren on the horizon yet?

By now Jerry's defences will have been lowered a bit more and so oiled with a few laughs and a few smiles along the way, the dialogue should now be flowing freely enough.

Once the uneasy part has passed you can begin to turn the conversation back to work.

'You know Jerry I would really like you to be my No1, I really do value your experience and I think we could work very well together to make this the best operation in the area.'

As the conversation flows, you can then slide in, 'Do you know Jerry, I've been going through some of the KPIs for your department and some of them really need to be looked at seriously. Wastage for a start, its running way above budget and it's driving the margin down. Now I know that things have not been easy for you lately, what with staff sickness and Lulu being on maternity leave, but we can't just let it run at that level now can we?'

Jerry will have some comments (excuses) to make and you must reply along these lines; 'Yes Jerry, I understand that, but you know and I know that if we were to focus on it and get the staff to focus on it that we could change it. Let me tell you something Jerry. My aim is to see this store at No1 in the Region. Just imagine that, good old Sunnybridge store at No1 in the Region!'

Jerry will most probably grudgingly agree, so time now for the 'killer' move.

Next thing is to bring up the specific point that was the last straw!

'Jerry, remember last week when I wanted to change the delivery times of ambient goods? I really screwed up on that one because being new, I hadn't realised it would clash with the new times for frozen goods.'

'Question is Jerry, why didn't you warn me?'

You don't need to wait for the answer, just continue. 'We need to build a team here Jerry and what we can't afford is for someone as capable as you not really being onside. I know you have a World of experience Jerry and the staff like you. I'd like to invite you to step over the line and be my No1, because I know that together we can really get things moving, are you with me?'

Hopefully he will agree. Now the way forward is to hold weekly meetings with Jerry where you will go through the previous week's figures and deal with aspects that are not where they need to be and also to discuss Head Office instructions and anything else that impacts on the business.

Once you have Jerry on side you will have the rest of the staff on side too because he's the unofficial 'Head Gnu!'

If that approach failed to work, and I have rarely known it not to, you must then explain the standards required and compare these with the actuality and where they fail to reach the mark then you must be prepared to go down the company's disciplinary route, because you cannot afford to have the likes of a negative Jerry holding the store *and* your future to ransom.

One final and most vital key...the confirmation e-mail!

When something important is agreed with a colleague or the boss, never be afraid to drop them a nice e-m to confirm matters and also to raise a file note regarding it.

Get into the habit and once you do your 'botty' will never be exposed.

As we pointed out at the very beginning of this book, it is quite possible that at some point you may come up against an unsavoury character either as a boss, a colleague or a subordinate.

Unsavoury bosses generally speaking are bullies who think that the best way of getting people to do what they want is to bully them, and when we refer to bullying in this context we mean mental abuse.

Anyone who is being bullied by a thug of a boss lives a life of misery whilst at work, and the bullying will continue until the abused person deals with the bully and this can be achieved by the process of assertion that we have described in this chapter.

CHAPTER 11

THE SUCCESS CALIBRATION

We can snapshot exactly how successful you will become in your management career based on your current Success Calibration.

If we were to do this today and the result did not impress you, take heart, because the result would only show the *current* position. As we know, progress is all about change and *becoming* that highly successful leader Manager that you aspire to become and the calibration will chart graphically exactly where you need to focus your attention in order to improve the calibration result in the future.

When it comes to human beings there is nothing new in the world and we can learn much from history and the figures that charted it, so at this juncture let's take a lesson from history and see a real live example of a phenomenal quantified Success Calibration.

We're going to travel back over 700 years to the 1300s. We're going to travel back to Scotland where we're going to meet Scotland's hero, William Wallace, and we're going to see how good old Braveheart himself unwittingly used the Success Calibration to calibrate sufficiently highly to achieve all those great deeds that got him into the history books!

Please be aware that whilst we have presented matters here in a humorous, light-hearted, tongue in cheek way....it *really* is serious stuff!

Most readers will have seen the Braveheart movie and it was a pretty good film with our hero portrayed so well by Mel Gibson, but the reality was even more exciting than the film. We only have anecdotal evidence of the small details that shaped Wallace's life from the poets and minstrels who lived at the time and it seems that Wallace was quite an ordinary guy, not very high born, but a member of a fairly well connected family.

Wallace's daddy was a minor nobleman who lived on the outskirts of what is now Glasgow, he had some retainers who worked on the land, he was a farmer, he grew crops, he raised animals and then he traded them in exchange for money. In other words they lived the simple life.

His son William would have worked in the family farming business 700 years ago as well, and if the leading Scottish nobles of the day hadn't squabbled amongst themselves like spoiled, greedy, selfish egotistical brats about who should wear the crown of Scotland, then Wallace would probably have lived and died on the farm a complete unknown.

History tells us that the Scottish nobles *did* squabble and to settle the argument they were stupid enough to invite King Edward from down south in England to come up and decide which of them should get the crown.

Big mistake! A bit like inviting a wolf to look after the sheep!

Before we go any further then, let's look at the other individual who played one of the lead roles on the stage of life at that time, King Edward.

He was a guy in his fifties and he was one of Europe's most powerful military rulers. He had already conquered great swathes of France by the sword, he was an accomplished general, and he had an army of tens of thousands comprised of English soldiers backed up by a vast horde of professional mercenaries from other parts of Europe.

On top of all the military prowess, he was a highly experienced and cunning statesman, and if that wasn't already enough, he was also vastly rich!

Well as you can see, this guy really was a big cheese, and do you know what the crafty swine did? First, he 'allowed' himself to be pushed, apparently unwillingly into coming up to Scotland to decide who should be king.

The conversation probably *didn't* go quite like this!

'What *me* decide….you want *Me*? Oh, I'm not sure I could, I mean I'm just old Ed from London, are you sure you want *Me*? Oh very well then, tish and pish. Oh, all right then, if you really don't have anyone else to help you, and if you really, really insist, then I suppose I could take a quick run up the M1 and visit, but I can only stay for a few days mind you!'

Of course he went, he knew exactly what he was up for, this wily tactician saw this ruse as a way of taking Scotland for himself without ever striking a single blow, and he did it bit by bit, little by little in his wily, crafty, cunning way.

The e-mails and blogs (ho hum!!) of the day captured it all as it happened. His game plan was simple: Get in there on the pretence of helping the Scots, next meet the Scottish nobles over vast banquets. Get to know them, get them a bit 'pished', find the ones who might be up for a bit of bribery and corruption, dazzle them with chests full of English gold, invite them back on Sunday afternoon for tea and cakes, tie up the deal when

200

they were sober, pay them an up-front deposit of the vast sums promised, and then, to really seal the deal, blow their minds by promising them more lands in return for their obedience and co-operation!

Next step, gradually move up the English army and dot the garrisons all around the place on the pretext that someone neutral has to keep the peace between the squabblers and their supporters whilst the decision making process continued. Then, when the stranglehold is complete, then and only then, call all the nobles back together and announce that you've reached your decision and that after very carefully considering all the claims to the throne... that as a matter of fact... although it had never occurred to you to even consider it before, that you, Edward, have the very best claim of all!

The stage managed rousing cheers of the assembled nobles who were in Edward's pay echoed though the great hall. What a stroke...and it had worked!

Greed and ego are an awfully predictable human failing aren't they?

So at this point, on the one hand we've got Edward with lots of Scottish nobles in his pocket, garrisons in every town, thousands of soldiers, vast wealth, vast experience both militarily and politically, and on the other, striding across the stage set of life, we have William Wallace, a 25 year old nobody from nowhere with nothing!

Now just think about it. If you were standing 700 hundred years ago in Ladbroke's Betting Shop in Tavern Green, Edinburgh staring up at the screens to see the odds they would be giving on William Wallace's chance of success, 100,000 to 1 against perhaps? Anyway you get the picture, you would certainly not have wagered one single groat on William Wallace, now would you?

Anyway, we'll come back to what happened between them later, meanwhile back to our assertion that we really can determine the degree of success you can expect based on your *current* calibration.

For more than a decade we've delivered seminars to over 300,000 people all around Europe, from England, Ireland, Scotland and Wales to Germany, Holland and Switzerland, and we can tell you that an individual's capacity for success or failure can be determined mathematically by a formula that we have developed over the years based on real life experience... and it's never failed to be 100% dead right!

We call it the 'Phoenix Calibration.' The reason? Because once you understand it, you can apply it to raise yourself, phoenix like, from whatever condition your management career is in now to the one you would like it to become in the future, the one that would assure your success.

Remember what the good news is? The good news is that you and I are free to put the values into the equation that we need to put in so we can get the results we want in the future!

Ready for this fabulous success equation?

$$S = \frac{N \times (Fs + Fb.e)}{Neg\ A} \times E$$

Where:

S = Success

N = Needs

Fs = Faith in Self

Fb.e = Faith in own business concept or employer

Neg A = Degree of negative attitude (Default setting / Government in power)

E = Effort

We're going to chart Braveheart's progress as he quite unwittingly began to put the values into own his personal success calibration equation, values that would go on to determine the phenomenal outcome he achieved over a few short years until he was betrayed by one of his own countrymen and sent to London for execution.

Isn't it amazing that a guy who lived over 700 years ago unwittingly used the very same success equation we're going to use to help you to succeed today? Isn't it amazing that every single great leader and achiever since the dawn of time quite unwittingly has used this very same equation to achieve his or her success!

Before we get on to Braveheart's details, we'd better get a bit of a foundation in place by looking at some imaginary illustrations a bit closer to home from amongst some character types you might all know quite well.

First, let's take good old Jason!

Jason is 27 years of age, left school at 15, drifted in and out of jobs, none of which have been anything more exciting than basic store warehousing jobs and all at minimum wage. He lives with his partner Linda, she is 23 and together they had a child, a child that they didn't plan, one that Jason would really prefer that he didn't have to think about, especially when it cries in the night, or when he's watching football! They live in a small flat in a poor area of town and they can't afford to run a car.

Not so good!

Anyway, let's start to input Jason and Linda's numbers into their personal success formula, starting with their 'N' factor….that's 'N' = NEED.

Well, what are their needs? Basically to have enough money to pay the rent and the basics like food and to pay for their Sky TV subscription because watching soaps is Linda's pleasure and football on Sky Sports is the highlight of Jason's week. In other words, enough money to buy the essentials and just get by and hopefully have enough left over to buy a cheap case of beer from the supermarket on Friday night for the weekend.

So for the sake of our formula, values run on a scale of 1 – 10 and as Jason and Linda do not have any big need at all in the general scale of things, let's put a factor of 2 in the 'N' NEED box. Remember the formula? Here it is once again:-

$$S = \frac{N \times (Fs + Fb.e)}{Neg\ A} \times E$$

Right then, moving onto the brackets, we have two 'F' values, first we have 'Fs', which is FAITH in SELF, and 'Fb.e' which is FAITH either in 'b' your own business, or 'e' the company you work for.

So in Jason's case as an employed person, 'e' stands for employer.

Let's begin by putting a value in Jason's 'Fs' box. Would you expect our character Jason to have much faith and confidence in himself?

No, not much. He hasn't achieved anything really significant in his life except to prove he can father a baby! He has never held a job down for long and has drifted in and out of work for 12 years.

So what should we give him as a confidence in self value, another 2 perhaps? So 'Fs' is a 2.

What about faith in his employer? Well people who come from Jason's neighbourhood all see employers as b*sta*ds out to screw the employees out of as much as possible. Jason hates bosses, he's like Homer Simpson;

the bell rings and he drops the white hot ingot right where he's standing at that precise moment and rushes out of the door to go home and watch TV.

He trips over the doorstep into work right on the button in the morning, and flies out of the door right on the button at night. Jason will steal as much time as possible in the toilet, he will take extra minutes on his break, and talking of taking things, when no-one is looking, he will take whatever he thinks he can get away with, including toilet paper. The boss owes him you see!

So what value shall we put in 'Fe'? You could be honest and say zero because Jason really hates his employer, but we'll be generous today and load up another 2.

So now above the line we have 2 + 2 which our calculator tells us adds up to 4.

Moving now below the line, what about the 'Neg A' value which is the degree of negative attitude Jason carries with him as his normal default setting which of course determines the shade of his government in power?

Well it's not too hard to see that Jason has a pretty negative default setting and his government in power has some stinking policies! He hates his job and his life is made tolerable only by the beer and Sky Sports at weekends, so on a scale of 1-10 what shall we mark him?

Well, he is *very* negative isn't he, but he isn't quite suicidal... so let's load up a 7!

The 'E' box is the multiplier box, and records the degree of effort Jason is willing to put in to achieve his needs. How much effort does he need to put in to achieve those needs? The answer is very, very little. In fact as far as Jason is concerned, as little as possible, so we can load up yet another 2 and drop that into the 'E' box.

So to calculate Jason's success calibration we have 2 x 4 = 8 above the line, divided by 7 from below the line which makes 1.1. We must now multiply this by Jason's 'E' factor which is 2. So now, having calculated it all out we find that Jason's success calibration… is a staggering 2.2!

Let's now compare this to Neil's success calibration. Neil is also 27; he went to the same school as Jason, left at the same age as Jason and started work in the same stockroom of the same retail store as Jason.

Now for the differences! Neil has always works hard, always arrives early for work and always works on beyond the time he is paid for.

When he first started he was noticed by his supervisor as an individual who took a serious interest in his work, who was always doing extra things and asking questions and so soon he was noticed by the boss and was offered a promotion to supervisor.

He continued to learn and do well, was sent on courses and was promoted to his current position which is Assistant Department Manager.

Neil lives with his wife Jane and their two little girls in an end terrace house they bought a couple of years ago on a mortgage. They keep their little garden tidy and Jane always keeps the house really nice and comfortable. They have a small car and always manage to save enough to take a little holiday every summer.

Neil wants to progress within the company so he can earn more and buy a bigger house in a better area, so the girls can go to a better school. He wants to provide more and better for his family and so he and Jane are quite prepared to work hard to achieve it.

Let's see how Neil's success calibration came out!

$$S = \frac{N \times (Fs + Fb.e)}{Neg\ A} \times E$$

What about Neil's 'N' box?

Well we know he wants to move to a better area to a better house and a better school so his little girls get a better chance in life, and we also know that he and Jane are prepared to work hard to achieve it.

We hope you agree that it would be fair to slot in an 8 into Neil's 'N' box.

What about the 'F' boxes?

Neil has worked hard, invested in himself by going on courses and learning, he has been promoted twice and so he has quite a degree of confidence in himself, so let's put another 8 into the 'Fs' box.

How about the 'Fe' box? Well Neil has a lot of faith in his employer, he sees himself as more than just a worker, he sees himself more as a partner because his boss has invested in him and he feels he has a notional ownership of the business, so let's slap in another 8!

Below the line?

Well Neil is mostly upbeat and positive, and so therefore is his Government in power, but from time to time he gets a run of the blues, so let's load up a 2 in the 'NEG A' box.

Now, turning to 'E' for effort.

Both he and Jane are prepared to do whatever they need to do to get that better home and better school, so we'll load up a 9!

Computing it all, we have 8 x (8+8) = 128 above the line, a 2 below the line, which leaves 64 to be multiplied by Neil's 9 for 'E' effort, so we arrive at a success calibration for Neil of 576, which is just a little better than Jason's amazing 2.2 now isn't it?

These are extreme examples that we have invented to illustrate the point, however although we have invented them, we all know a Jason and Linda and a Neil and Jane don't we?

The most important thing at this moment is for *you* to recognise where *you* are. Please don't kid yourself, be honest because if you're not, the only person you'll cheat is the man in the mirror!

213

A very important point here.

When you load up your scores to calculate your own calibration, please don't use the ones you felt *after* your most recent success! No, we are talking here about your *norm* because what is crucial and essential is never to be erratic, but consistently constant and to use norm values for calculation purposes...or you'll fool yourself!

If you have been honest, which we hope you have, and you aren't impressed, then interpret the results, draw some conclusions and make the decision to change by working on areas of weakness to make them into strengths!

Now let's see what happened to our Scottish Superhero William Wallace, and then we'll draw some conclusions and see how we can help you get your own calibration maxed and working powerfully for you too!

Let's begin with the first value in Wallace's formula, 'N' need.

What was Wallace's need and how much value did he put into his need box? Need is a very important factor indeed, in fact it is possibly THE most important factor in the entire equation because if you think about it, 'need' translates into desire which translates into 'motive', which in turn can be expressed as motivation, which then breaks down into 'motive - for - action'. So if you have low needs then you will have low motivation, correspondingly if you have high needs then you will have high motivation and therefore a far higher chance of achieving your aims and goals... compare Jason and Neil to prove the point!

We're going to look back in a very tongue in cheek way at Braveheart's experience, but please don't take the satirical events described here too seriously!!

Looking back to the precise ins and outs of things that happened 700 years ago is never going to be very easy, especially in this case, because some dozy monk pressed 'delete' instead of 'save' by mistake on the blogs of the day, and we lost the entire blog of that whole period, including some rather spectacular videos of hand to hand combat!

Anyway, apparently what happened was something like this…ho hum!!:

Wallace was a young 25 year old 'man about town' and his local town was Lanark, which is just south of Glasgow. Wallace used to nip into Lanark with his buddies on Friday and Saturday nights after they all got paid, and go round the taverns and nightclubs. They'd have a few pints of ale in each tavern, play a few a games of hazard (a gambling game of the period) and then move on to Ye Golden Groat Nightclubbe to watch the local maidens dancing to all the latest hit madrigals, then he'd go home in the early hours of the morning more than a little pished, much I might add, to Mrs Wallace's annoyance!

As you might guess, there was always a bit of tension between the locals and the soldiers from the English Army Garrison who were always after the women and were often drunk in the town and starting fights outside the nightclubs and taverns. Well on one particular night, Wallace and his mates were in town, they'd been round the taverns, they'd finished up at Ye Golden Groat Nightclubbe where they'd had more than just a few Jager Bombs to finish off the night, and when they came out to go home they saw a group of English soldiers having a happy slapping session with an old Scottish couple, and the worst of it was that one of the soldiers was even recording it all on his mobile phone!

Well as you can imagine, seeing this, Wallace instantly flew into an incandescent alcohol fuelled rage and waded in to the fray with his pals.

There was a massive fight and Wallace killed one of the soldiers.

Now here's the twist! The guy who got killed just happened to be the son of Hesselrig, the Governor of Lanark! When Wallace realised whom he had killed he legged it home like a racehorse on dope where his wife was waiting up for him on the doorstep, rolling pin in hand!

He explained to her what had happened and I can only say that she really laid into him, really let rip. Reminded him of how often she had implored him not to go out round the bars, how often she had begged him not to drink too much, get drunk and get into fights, how often she had begged him not to antagonise the soldiers, and now this had happened!

Anyway, they went to bed and made up, but in the early hours of the morning Wallace was woken up by a text message on his mobile phone to warn them that Hesselrig himself had not only seen the happy slapping video, but also the fight and knew exactly who had killed his son, and that he was on the way at that very moment to get Wallace and bring him to justice!

Sure enough, half an hour later who should come clanking up the drive but Hesselrig at the head of a squad of armed English Soldiers all clad in that fashionable silver grey chain mail armour of the day!

This was no time to show off his sword skills, so Wallace quickly nipped out of the back door telling his wife he would hide in the big tree in the garden, shouting over his shoulder to get rid of them as quickly as possible.

Hesselrig banged his chain mailed fist on the door, Mrs Wallace eventually opened it, he demanded to see Wallace, she said he wasn't in, hadn't seen him all night, didn't know where he was and didn't know when he'd be back.

Well, as you can imagine, under the circumstances Hesselrig was more than just a little bit miffed, and he wasn't about to be messed around with by a mere slip of a girl! So, drawing his sword to prove he meant business, he asked her again, but again she refused. In a fit of rage, 'swish' went the sword, and in the blink of an eye she lay dead and bleeding on the doorstep!

Once Hesselrig had gone, Wallace came down from the tree, went back to the house to find the awful scene before him on the doorstep. He couldn't believe his eyes! There was his precious wife, brutally murdered, dead and bleeding on the doorstep and it was all his fault!

Wallace was gripped by a volatile mixture of the most powerful of all human emotions it is possible to experience; grief, rage, love, regret, loss, blame, hatred and an all-consuming desire for vengeance!

Ok then, let's step out of the story for a moment. Ask yourself, have you ever looked back on your life and identified a single pivotal point in it, a point that changed everything forever, because nothing was ever the same again after that point?

This episode in Wallace's life was for him that powerful pivotal point, and from this point on nothing in his life was ever going to be the same again. All of a sudden he was transformed from a Jason type character by this powerful motive for action, a motive that changed him from being a bit of an irrelevant waste of space into the total fulfilment of his potential.

This dreadful incident began to pile up a massive value into Wallace's 'N' NEED box!

This massive, massive build-up of the most powerful emotions that it is possible for a human being to experience began to focus Wallace on a single, all-consuming desire. Now, for the first time in his life he had a real purpose! He made an irrevocable covenant with himself; to rid Scotland of Edward, to rid Scotland of every single one of the thousands of occupying soldiers that blighted his country, to rid Scotland of every single one of Edward's paid Scottish snouts who had betrayed their country in return for English gold, and in the process of doing all this, to put a rightful Scottish king on the throne.

He vowed that he would achieve this, or die in the struggle to achieve it.

Now that is what we call commitment!

So there you have the plot laid out before you. He, William Wallace, a 25 years old nobody from nowhere was going to get rid of King Edward and all that he stood for and this was going to be his sole reason for waking in the morning, for breathing and for eating and drinking.

The attainment of that single objective was his sole reason for living.

Think about it. No big deal was it? A really simple task for a 25 year old nobody who came from nowhere and had nothing! A really simple task, to take on one of Europe's most powerful military rulers, to take on the might of the entire English army, foreign mercenaries and all. A simple task for a 25 year old nobody who didn't even have any men to fight for him!

Well when we fully investigate all that happened over the next few years to Wallace, Edward and Scotland, it isn't too hard to see how all it takes to make history is *one* person. *One* person with the right degree of 'N' who is prepared to passionately commit everything to his cause....even his own life.

Ghandi is another rather more peaceful example!

As we know, Wallace not only drove the English out, but his army almost got to London before they turned back to go home and take in the harvest! Not a bad result for a 25 year old nobody from nowhere was it?

Obviously, he could not have achieved all that he achieved alone, he needed other people and thousands of them, people who were prepared to die for the cause for which he had filled them with passion!

When he began his mission, his circle of power contained only one person, himself, however in a very short period of time he was able to extend his circle of power and create a circle of influence so that in the end thousands flocked to join him.

So how did Wallace go about extending his circle of influence and attracting the people he needed? Well for a start he became a charismatic leader, you *have* to be a charismatic leader if you are going to persuade people to join you in an enterprise, even though they know that there is a distinct chance they'll be butchered in the process!

You might say, 'Well that counts me out then, no way am I charismatic.' Not so fast! People are not born charismatic, they *become* charismatic. How? Well, to become charismatic you must have a vision, and we don't mean the pot puffing type! As a leader manager the vision you might hold is perhaps how you want your operation to perform, how you want it to look and how you want it to feel, rather like Nancy in the earlier chapter when she took over an Area that was virtually on the skids, and in a few short months changed it into a highly motivated team of go-getters who together achieved the No1 spot in less than 12 months from a position of 67 out of 72!

Once you have that vision crystal clear in your mind, the next step is to share that vision with other people in a highly dynamic and passionate way so that they become, like you, fully charged and totally committed to achieving the vision you shared with them.

It's a bit like having a cold; you can't infect someone else with a cold unless you yourself are infected with it first! So you need to be fully 'infected' with enthusiasm and passion for your vision so that you can 'infect' other people and motivate them to buy into the vision and join you in working to make it a reality.

We are quite certain that Wallace didn't sit round with his friends, all morose and miserable and say, 'Aye, it'd be affa good tae see those Sassenachs awaa fae here, ye ken, but we canna do anything abooot it. (big sigh) Naa, we'll just have to put up with it and accept them being here!'

On the contrary, we're quite sure he was filled with a great degree of highly charged motivation, and being so highly motivated himself, he was able to motivate others to share his vision.

Motivation breaks down into motive – for – action remember, and that's what he gave them, a deeply powerful motive for action, even though it meant facing death!

225

In the scenario we gave of Nancy's drive to Number 1, we saw that she gave her team the vision, she shared what it would be like to *be* the Number 1 team, the pride they could take, the prizes they would win, the recognition they would receive and the financial rewards they would earn.

Let's get back to Wallace's success calibration!

We thought Neil's was pretty good, certainly in comparison with Jason's, so let's see how Wallace's stacks up!

$$S = \frac{N \times (Fs + Fb.e)}{Neg\ A} \times E$$

We've already said his 'N' NEED box is maxed out because he was prepared to die for it, so let's give him a 10.

How about his 'F' FAITH box? Do you think he had faith in himself? I think that anyone who seriously set out to do what he did must have total and unerring faith in himself, not only that, total and unerring faith in his team. He had no employer, so we can't use that, but instead we'll use faith in his enterprise or mission. I'm sure you'd agree that both of these should also be a 10.

So now, on the top line we have 10 x (10 + 10) = 200.

What about under the line, 'NEG A,' degree of negative attitude? This really means of course, what is the shade of his mental government in power?

Well Wallace was human after all, and I'm sure that there were many times when his plans didn't work out the way he wanted them to. As the leader, there must have been many times when he sat alone in the wee small hours of the morning, staring into the last flickers from the dying embers of his fire. At times like these he would have had to fight very hard against the Misery Party who would have tried their level best to plant the seeds of self-doubt in his mind as they tried to take over as his mental government in power. I'm certain he did not give in to these, but as he wasn't perfect we can't give him a zero, but we can give him a 1!

How about 'E' EFFORT? Well, we can't give a guy any less than 10 who applied every waking moment of his life, not just for a few weeks, but over several years to achieving his aim!

So where does Wallace finish up? He has 200 above the line and 1 below the line, well according to my calculator 200 divided by 1 is 200, so now we'll multiply that by the 10 in the 'E' box and Wallace calibrates at a staggering 2000!

So we have the amazing Jason who calibrates at 2.2 and nowhere near the 'Performance Zone' calibration which we believe starts at 500. The Performance Zone is the place you need to be in order to achieve results!

Neil calibrated at 576 which puts him in the Performance Zone, but William Wallace is the absolute winner with an outstanding calibration of 2000, right there close to the centre of the Performance Zone!

It isn't difficult to sift through the factors that separated Neil from Jason and Neil from the epitome, Wallace. Jason put NOTHING in, Neil put quite a lot in, but Wallace put EVERYTHING in!

That reminds us of the story of the pig and the hen. The story goes that all the animals on Farmer Giles' farm were all very, very happy with the way the farmer looked after them, in fact they wanted for nothing!

One day the hen was perched on the wall of the pig's sty and the pig and the hen were chatting about how good life was on Farmer Giles' farm, and they agreed it was perfect!

They then got to discussing how they could do something really nice to pay the farmer back. They fell silent and then suddenly the hen let out an excited squawk! 'I've got a fantastic idea,' she said, 'How about this! Why don't we give him a really nice cooked breakfast? I can supply the eggs and you can supply the bacon!'

The pig thought for a moment then replied, 'Hmm, all *you* would have to do is lay some eggs, *I* would have to give a slice of myself!'

Interesting story!

If you are standing on the edge of the vast plain that is your career in management, gazing into the far distance at mist shrouded Success Mountain, then you must accept that hens never make it, but pigs do because they are prepared to commit *themselves* totally to achieving their goal...a place high up on success mountain!

So decide...are you going to be a hen or a pig?

Back to *your* calibration!

If you cheat, then the only person you cheat will be yourself. We strongly recommend that before you sit down to work out your own calibration you go somewhere quiet and create what we call your 'need' list.

Remember this is what goes into the 'N' box, this is what creates the motivation, this is the starting point, this is the driver of your success. Jason had small needs and so needed small effort and in turn small 'success' in order to fulfil them, on the other hand Wallace had vast needs and needed great effort and in turn great success to fulfil them. It is most certainly a very worthwhile investment of time to do this exercise properly and we strongly suggest that you do not undertake this flippantly, but since your future depends on it, do it seriously!

Before we move on from this topic, a few more words on 'need.'

'It would be ok having an xyz...I wouldn't mind having an xyz...I would like an xyz...I would love an xyz...I want an xyz...I must have an xyz...I will have an xyz.'

If each statement was made by a different speaker, which of them would you expect to be the proud owner of an xyz in due course?

Obviously only the last two speakers are in any way deadly serious and a deadly serious objective that you are emotionally connected with in a highly enthusiastic way is the only level of emotion that will create a powerful enough vision to register positive data with the Universe, draw others into your circle of influence and so contribute to your success as it begins to manifest into your reality.

Imagine for a moment being a parent, and behind a locked door your child is screaming that the room is on fire.

You have no key, so what can you do? Just say perhaps, 'Well I'd like to get you out Sweetheart, but sorry, I don't have a key.'

We don't think so, because if the worst came to the worst there would be a dad or mum shaped hole in the door and the child would be out in a heartbeat!

That level of desire; nothing will stop you...is the level of desire that once focussed with passion and commitment, will achieve miracles!

If your score is not enough to get you into the performance zone then take an honest look at yourself and be prepared to make the changes necessary to get yourself into the zone...remember the only person standing between you and your success is YOU!

CHAPTER 12

ALL ABOUT BUSINESS

You will recall that we defined 'management' as:

Management comprises planning, organising, staffing, leading, directing, and controlling an organisation (a group of one or more people or entities) or effort for the purpose of accomplishing a goal.

We have spent a great deal of time discussing the 'people' elements of management simply because this is the most difficult aspect to get right!

If you had to operate your business with robots and not humans, they would operate according to their design parameters and all you would need to do is get them regularly serviced and if they began to falter and not churn out the finished product in the quantity required, then you would have them fixed…or if the repair was uneconomic to carry out, you'd have them scrapped and replaced!

In comparison with humans, robots would never aspire to be the best, would not be competitive, would not be jealous, would not connive, would not steal, would not be lazy, would not be untruthful, would not need to be motivated, would not pull a 'sickie', would not need to be trained, would not have mood swings, would not have lives outside work that could impact inside work, would not get angry, would not leave for a promotion, would not storm out, would have no likes or dislikes, would have no ambition.

We humans however, have all these potentials and many more, and this is the reason that we have spent so much time on the people aspect of management, as it is through people that you will succeed or fail!

Let's now turn to the other dynamic of business management, the numbers, but before we do let's discuss another quality the Leader Manager possesses!

The Leader Manager knows what's going on everywhere in his operation.

How?

Something that must be learned early on in your management career is that an effective manager does *not* live in an ivory tower remote from the 'coal face.' Equally, neither does he or she live in the machine shop or sales floor, because someone has to be up on the bridge guiding the ship!

How he or she can effectively control both ends of the equation is through two processes, one is called 'inspection' whilst the other is called 'walking the job,' both of which are highly effective control systems and communication tools!

Let's start with inspection. It is always amazing that when we walk into a retail store for example, we may find the store fascia dirty, the paint flaking, weeds growing out of the wall/pavement joint, entrance doors dirty, whilst inside the store price tickets are missing, equipment is dusty and there is what we call 'impedimenta,' aka rubbish, on the checkouts.

Why is this? Simply because the manager is not carrying out a daily inspection, and we don't mean 'Ok the counters are still there, the tills are still there, job done!' No, we mean starting outside with a clip board looking to see what the customers see as their first impression (you can only make one first impression!) and then moving inside aisle by aisle until the entire store has been inspected. From the inspection list can be decided what is urgent and immediate that must be attended to first and what can wait until later.

John's car went in a garage for a check recently, these were the premises of a national group, however when John went into the 'mot viewing area,' he was appalled by the general litter, grime and filth evident throughout all the service bays leading to the thought, 'If they don't care about their own environment can I trust them to care about my car?' This place cannot have been inspected formally for months, so bit by bit standards gradually dropped, and now, because it has become the norm, the manager had become oblivious to it.

Inspections are an essential key to achieving and maintaining high quality standards. If this is not done formally then, just by entering the business day in and day, out the manager eventually becomes oblivious to the deterioration in standards. It's a little like the window wipers in the car. You don't realise how bad they are until you fit new ones!

Next, 'walking the job.' Subordinates often tell you what they think you want to hear, which is not always the reality, also they will not always place the same level of priority on certain items as you, the Manager does, so you need a system for bypassing roadblocks to get to the truth and to ensure that information is quickly and effectively getting to those who must use it.

Imagine for example, that you are the manager of a manufacturing business and the Board has recently issued a new policy regarding the manufacture of a certain product. You communicated this new policy directly to your subordinates on Monday morning and so on Tuesday afternoon you 'walk the job.'

This means you go into the machine shop, or the place things are manufactured, and as you pass by Jim on the metal press you stop and ask how he's getting on. You then ask him how the new operating system is working.

He looks at you blankly, 'What new system?'

You explain that you'll get Dave, his supervisor to run through the operating system documentation with him later on.

Next stop, Dave the supervisor!

You ask Dave the same question you asked Jim. Like Jim he looks blank, so you tell him that you'll get Tony, his Manager over to go through the details.

Next stop Tony, the Assistant Manager!

The same process is repeated and Tony tells you he knows about it but just hasn't had time to tell Dave yet.

Now that you've found the blockage, you need to dislodge it!

Tony's manager Chris, is clearly not checking back to see that his instructions are being carried out and when you confront him, he tells you he told Dave but Dave obviously didn't do it.

You can handle this is several ways. The positive way is to say, 'Tony, suppose I told you that you were going to get a pay rise this month, but when the month end came it had not happened and so you complained to me about it. I then told you I had forgotten to tell the wages department, how would you feel? Well that's how I feel now Tony, best get onto it right away and confirm it has been done'

The negative way is to say, 'Tony if I have to come down here to make sure the message has got through, then I don't need you, best sharpen up because we don't employ name badges.'

Tony has now had a 'kick up the ass!'

You need to follow that up with a bit of staff training, where you can explain the essential element that once an instruction has been issued to a subordinate that we should never assume it will done, but that they must *confirm* it has been done.

When we assume, it makes an *ass* of *u* and *me!*

There are other benefits however. When you talk to Jim you can get his input as the operator on how things can be done better, more efficiently, quicker or at less cost…you can also talk to him about the level of waste being experienced in the machine shop…all of which affects the bottom line profit of the business you run, a subject we're going to discuss next!

We define the term 'business' in the context of this book as a mechanism through which money is made (not by the Royal Mint) and basically, in order to make money items must be either manufactured or obtained, or services delivered and then sold to consumers at a price greater than the cost price. It is the function of the Manager then to control the business environment in such a way that losses within the process are minimised and gains are maximised.

Obviously this is a simplistic observation as we have made no mention of the 'black arts' carried out behind the locked doors of the Sales and Marketing Department for example, and we have no intention of listening at the door!

We will confine ourselves to explaining the control systems through which the Manager can monitor the essential elements of the business that will ensure the business is as profitable as possible.

'When your outgo exceeds your income your upkeep will be your downfall.'

A simple but accurate summary that is as true of private lives as in businesses, accordingly the devising and implementation of effective business control systems is essential.

The most important document is the budget.

This document contains all the financial details of the business for the year in question and it follows that if the manager can ensure that the business achieves or exceeds these numbers then the budgeted bottom line profit figure will also be achieved or exceeded.

In order to create a budget for the business, the Board, or top management team, will look at the previous year's performance, quantify and include all known factors that are likely to impact on the business, either negatively or positively in the coming year and include a factor for growth and make absolutely sure that the profit contribution reaches required return on investment criteria.

Obviously, all businesses are a 'live' entity and since nobody has a crystal ball to see into the future, the budget represents the best view that can be taken *at the time*, however situations and events are likely to occur during the year to come that were not included in the budget since they were unknown at that time, and it is how the manager reacts to these situation or events as the weeks go by, that will mark his or her success or failure.

The budget is really a 'promissory note' that illustrates to the Head Office, shareholders and also lenders perhaps, where the business will be financially at the year end.

Within the budget are fixed costs and variable costs. Fixed costs are the things the Manager cannot control, such as rent or council tax for example, whilst variable costs are those costs that are within the Manager's every day control; wage cost (e.g. accurate staff cover forecasting), gross margin (e.g. strict control of wastage etc) and energy costs (e.g. turns the lights off) and it is on these things that the sharp and effective Manager will focus, whilst the slack manager will let things slide so that bottom line profit falls back.

Once the budget document is completed and the figures broken down into weekly, monthly or 4 weekly slices, it then becomes that promissory note that it is the Manager's responsibility to fulfil, and of course achievement or non-achievement is a major performance criterion against which the Manager's performance will be measured. Hit or exceed the profit numbers and everyone is happy, miss them and the Manager's performance is seriously under the microscope!

This is where the Manager must become 'drum tight and razor sharp,' which is the title of one of our management development seminars, if he or she is to be effective in producing the results required. So much depends on it!

Most businesses monitor results on daily or weekly basis and produce a Profit and Loss Account (P&L) monthly to measure against the budget in order to effectively control it. The P&L is laid out in precisely the same way as the budget, so it becomes an easy task to enter the actual figures against the budgeted figures. At this point we can add a 3rd and 4th column so that we can show the cash variance, either positive (hopefully!) or negative, and the final column which expresses the + or - variance against budget as a percentage.

The use of percentages allow ratios to be used to control and monitor performance against budget, this is a far more effective means of controlling the business than the use of straight cash or unitary amounts. Suppose, for example the budget shows £15,000 as the cash wage cost for the month of March, or Period 3 if using a 13 x 4 week calendar, however the actual wage cost is £16,000 indicating a £1000 overspend.

Is the overspend due to slack management?

Perhaps not! If we investigate further we may see, for argument's sake, that the budgeted labour to turnover ratio is 20% against a budgeted turnover of £75,000 however the *actual* turnover was £88,000, a 15% increase above budget. If we then look at the actual situation we will see that in order to achieve this 15% increase it was necessary to employ more staff and the result was that the actual labour to turnover ratio was 18.8%.

Here we can see that the 'overspend' is actually justified because, whilst the budgeted turnover was £75,000 with a labour to turnover *ratio* of 20%, the actual turnover was £88,000 at a *ratio* of only 18.8%, an improvement in performance of 1.2 percentage points.

So does the Manager get a kick or a pat on the back? Hopefully the latter!

On the other hand, however, if turnover is not meeting budget expectation we must be prepared to reduce wage cost back to the budget labour to turnover ratio whilst we search for a solution to rectify the turnover shortfall.

This rationale can be applied to just about every variable cost, since all variable costs are, for the most part, eventually a ratio relationship with turnover.

Now for the interesting bit!

Once the actual performance for the month or period has been entered into the 'actual' column of the control document and negative variances highlighted in red, the results can be evaluated by the manager who will be sensitive not only to negative variances, but also the trends that will build up as the months go by.

Why is turnover down on budget? If we are a retail operation, is it because we are not keeping the store full and mounting effective promotions. If we are a sales

247

organisation, are the Sales Representatives performing at the level required?

Why is turnover up on budget? Is there a trend that shows that every third week there is a surge in turnover? Why is this, what can we do to capitalise on it?

Why is the physical cost of sales higher than budget? Is it because turnover is over budget and more raw material or product was required to achieve this?

Why are energy costs over budget? Did we require more energy to meet increased production, or if not are we carelessly wasting energy?

Why is turnover down on budget?

Imagine your business is like a patient on the operating table, hooked up to all the dials and readouts that show the medical team the patient's vital signs that they need to monitor as the operation proceeds and warn them should an intervention become necessary if things begin to go wrong.

Your business is hooked up to the P&L versus budget, which clearly shows all the vital signs.

Should you notice a negative variance this will need to be attended to quickly as it will have reduced the bottom line for the month or period in question. The variance must be fully investigated by the manager and corrective action taken to ensure that there is no repeat next month, and if possible a way must be found to recoup the loss!

Budget and P&L are not actually the financial control system's 'Dynamic Duo,' in fact it really is a case of the 'Dynamic Trio,' because the third element is the Year End Forecast which is updated based on actuality as the months go by.

Here we take the actual results achieved against budget each month and project this forward using the appropriate parameters to project an updated forecast which will show either an improved or worsening position against budget.

If the position is improved then no problemo...however if it is worse than budget, best get busy on finding a solution before its too late!

When it comes to budgets and P&Ls, I think Rudyard Kipling (30 December 1865 – 18 January 1936) and his book 'The Elephant's Child' contains some excellent advice to Managers on the questions that should be asked during a variance investigation, and he made up this little rhyme as a memory jogger.

I keep six honest serving-men:
(They taught me all I knew)
Their names are What and Where and When
And How and Why and Who.

This can be developed as follows:-	
Place:	Where is it done?
	Why is it done there?
	Where else might it be done?
	Where should it be done?
Sequence:	When is it done?
	Why is it done then?
	When might it be done?
	When should it be done?

Person:	Who does it?
	Why does that person do it?
	Who else might do it?
	Who should do it?
Means:	How is it done?
	Why is it done that way?
	How else might it be done?
	How should it be done?

The P&L and budget documents should never be treated as 'dead,' but as the heartbeat of the business, because that is exactly what they are. They will clearly signpost to you where you should be looking and what you should be attending to in order to keep things smoothly on track to the end of the financial year, so you get a pat on the back, a good appraisal for outstanding performance and hopefully a pay rise too rather than a kick in the pants!

However, suppose you identify something that you, the manager, have no control over? Taking our retail store analogy, suppose a competitor decides to open up 4 doors down the High Street?

Things look tough, you've had your team together to see what ideas they have to help you compete with the new kid on the block. Together you come with some good ideas, however these are things you yourself cannot implement…however as you are a Leader Manager, you aren't just going to roll over, no, you are going to give these guys a run for their money!

Of course, as a Leader Manager, you not only have a circle of power remember, you also have a circle of influence, so you start to make calls to people who will help you. Reps for example who can arrange special price deals, Head office who can authorise price reductions on key things and strong customer incentives that you promote in order to stimulate business and fight the competition.

You know that your regular customers are bound to try out the competition, however you have always maintained an excellent relationship with them and you know they will be back because you have invested heavily in customer service which makes them feel valued and worthwhile. Not only that, your campaign is designed to bring in new customers whom you and your team will do your level best to make into regular customers.

Your plans begin to work and you see your figures gradually respond…the patient is going to pull through!

Not sure how well the Manager Manager would do under the same circumstances with just his circle of power to call on!

Now the next thing we need to do with our budget document and our P&L is to use it to forecast the end of year position. In that way we can update our year end position forecast every month and we can use it to guide us by the month to a successful year end figure.

John can vividly remember a former Director of his and how he treated people who were not fully in control of their business.

He would arrive quite out of the blue and ask the scared shitless manager an innocent question. 'How are you doing so far against last week?' If he waffled, he would then ask another more searching question, and if that too was answered unsuccessfully with a response such as 'I don't know,' then this would lead to a tirade of abuse where he would shout, 'What's your name? What day of the week is it? What year is it? You haven't a clue have you?' Always followed by, 'You are a complete waste of time, you are an excuse for a manager, I'm going out for 20 minutes and when I come back we're going to do a full profit review.'

He rolled his 'r's, so it was always a 'pwofit weview'. His 'pwofit weviews' were rather worse than a Gestapo interrogation, which if it did not go successfully, could and did frequently lead to, 'Wight, you haven't got a clue have you? Clear your desk, get out and find something else to do, you're in the 'wong' job!'

I have seen hard men reduced to tears because of this type of treatment, but of course in those days, and in that company, people were ruled by fear…and there was no such thing as a 'Tribunal' to appeal to of course!

Happy days!

The updated forecast for the year ahead is a vital tool to steer the business towards a positive outcome, and it is the task of the Manager to ensure that the numbers are achieved in order that the bottom-line profit for the year is also achieved.

You could view it as the route map which if followed faithfully will ensure the business will get safely from A to B.

So, let's imagine that the budget has been approved by the Board and has been passed to you the Manager to achieve.

You will see that across the year some costs remain the same and this is the case because they are fixed costs that the manager cannot influence, rent or business rates for example.

On the other hand there are costs over which the Manager has direct control, wage cost for example. Equally the Manager has a high degree of control over

255

the turnover of the business and it is the job of the Manager to ensure that the numbers are achieved and exceeded wherever possible.

Once again we can revert to the default setting and government in power in the mind of the Manager who opens the file containing the budget for the first time.

Those who have a negative government in power will immediately focus on the hike in turnover above last year that has been included in the budget, moan that it can't be done and then begin to start to think failure thoughts. On the other hand, those with a positive government in power will immediately pick up the challenge with a 'Can do.' attitude and get their team on side and motivate them to pick up the challenge.

Financial management is all about being aware, aware of what's going on physically, financially and personally!

CHAPTER 13

GOAL SETTING

Finally, we cannot leave the subject of Management without introducing the subject of goal setting and planning.

Another true adage, 'If you fail to plan, you plan to fail.'

Human beings are at heart very much goal seeking creatures, not all humans of course, we all know lazy people who just drift through life contributing nothing and achieving nothing.

A goal must consist of an aim or objective; a new business, a promotion, a new home, a new car, a specific holiday for example, anything you decide it should be in fact. If they are material things then they must be quantified by cost.

Whilst goals can relate to anything under the sun that we choose to make a goal, to be effective all goals must have one thing in common; a physical date by which they will be achieved.

The fact is, that without a date it isn't really a goal at all, it's just an idle wish. Your goals *must* be quantified and they *must* have a time by which they must be accomplished if you are to have any chance at all of using the process of goal setting to accelerate your progress to the top.

Imaging saying, 'My goal is to make a lot of money.'

Great, the only issue is, how will you know *when* you have reached your goal, since it has not been quantified?

Why *must* a goal have an end date by which time it must be achieved?

Without an end date there can be no focus, and without focus there can be no drive, no power and no commitment. Without an end date to aim for, the goal stands little chance of becoming a reality since it is merely an empty wish.

We always chatted to people during the interval at the seminars we spoke at and following a session on Goal Setting, John asked some delegates if they had goals. One man answered strongly, 'Oh yes, I've got a goal all right!'

'Ok great,' John replied, would you mind sharing it with us?'

'Well I've always fancied getting a Harley Davidson motorcycle, you know the type, black and all chrome with loud exhausts.'

'Wow, fantastic! How much will it cost you and when will you buy it? John was keen to know.

I, Nancy, had to freeze my expression because I knew what might well happen next!

'Er, well, to be honest I haven't got round to pricing one yet and I'm not really sure when I'll be able to get one.'

That went down like a lead balloon with John, and the simple fact was that this poor chap was deluding himself. He had no goal, it was just an idle wish that he kept in his mind with the attendant saying, 'One day.'

Sadly for him 'One day' is not on the calendar, so unless he wins the lottery…

So, a quantified goal with an end date is essential if you are to use the power of goal setting to help you achieve your objective, and the reason? Simple, because by setting an end date you introduce another resource, time!

You may never have considered this before, however time is the only finite resource you actually have. We all know the date and time the clock of our life was started, however we can't know the date and time it will stop, only that one day it *will* stop.

What that means is that we have to use that finite resource as effectively as possible and never waste a single hour of it, so we must do as much as we can *whilst* we can, and the most effective way of doing that is to have focus on a single objective at a time.

As an aside, this *does not* mean that you must become a 'workaholic' working every hour that God sends, because if you do, you will be existing in an out of balance life. In order to become truly successful, it is *essential* that you achieve the optimal work life balance so that you can actually live, rather than exist and in turn deliver your best performance consistently. So please do schedule time off, days out and nights out, or you *will* become jaded, dull and ineffective, which in turn will stop you being a sharp and effective Manager.

Consider a spinning top, the kind you may have got out of a Christmas cracker. We would hold it between finger and thumb, give it a sharp twist and let it spin away perfectly balanced on the table as if by magic, much to the delight of the little children.

Imagine for a moment however that the spinning top had a small piece missing from the edge of it. If you were to spin *this* top, it would do it's best to remain erect and spin according to the laws of physics, however that would be impossible because it is out of balance. All that would happen is that it would wobble crazily and career all over the table, gradually slowing down to fall over and go round in circles until the energy was exhausted and then it would finally stop.

The first top typifies a person with the correct work/life balance necessary to remain healthy and happy and successful, whilst the second typifies someone who is very much out of balance, a person who will eventually unravel, fall over and be utterly miserable in the process!

Decide *not* to be the personification of the second example.

So, back on the subject of goals; suppose the date set for the achievement of our overall goal is 3 years, two months and 3 days away. In order to achieve that overall goal we will inevitably have to achieve dated and quantified sub-goals along the way, each of which brings us one step closer to attaining the overall goal.

In order to be effective, we must focus on the next sub-goal in date order along the route *to the exclusion* of all else that might distract us, if we are to progress steadily forward.

In analogy, consider a magnifying glass, the type that we as children used to focus the power of the sun through to set things alight. We quickly learned if we were to start that fire then we *must* first *focus* the sun's rays into a tiny dot on the object, and then *hold it steady* until the smoke started and then the flame burst forth.

We would have achieved nothing if we failed to focus, and we would have achieved nothing if we kept moving the magnifying glass all the time, even if it was focused.

Apply the same rationale to your own goal. Focus your effort (sun's rays) steadily and consistently on each sub-goal until you set it on fire (achieve it) and then do the same thing on the next and the next and the next and ultimately, within the time frame selected you have set you will achieve your overall goal.

Imagine going on holiday and as you board the aircraft you turn left and not right, and you ask the Captain where he is taking you.

What would you think if he looked round and said, 'Weeeell, not too sure really, I'm going to kinda take off and climb to whatever height the plane decides to fly at, and then we'll just have to see where it takes us I suppose.'

If you had that conversation I think you would beat a hasty retreat down the steps and off the plane before they could slam the door!

Interesting isn't it? You expect the Captain of an airliner to know *exactly* where he is going, to know the *exact* course and height he will fly at and to have an estimated time of arrival at a specific destination...

Yet, when it comes to the *one life* we have some people seem content to drift along day by day with no specific goal in mind, curious that!

We hope we made the point loud and clear.

We all meet people in our lives, either at work or socially, who have a lifetime impact on us, John remembers one such person when he was an Area Manager for a leading UK supermarket chain.

This man was a very effective Manager and everything about him literally smelled of success. Although he was an Area Manager in a different division, John loved to be around him whenever their store visits coincided, so that he could and learn from him.

One day, when they were in a store office together, the phone rang and John's colleague answered it. After a very brief conversation, he pulled from the inside of his suit jacket, a small ultra slim leather bound book and slid out from the spine an equally ultra slim pen, and flipping the book open, he began to write.

John was curious and asking about it and learned it was a time management and personal effectiveness tool called a Day-Timer. John's colleague explained that by religiously using this tool he could plan effectively and *forget* nothing, all of which clearly contributed to his effectiveness.

John quickly bought one and found it invaluable in improving his own effectiveness also! Today there are a variety of electronic devices for achieving the same aim, 'forget ye not!'

Both John and his colleague went on to become Regional Executives within the company, however John's colleague eventually became a Director of this mega billion company, all of which goes to prove that planning and time management are essential components of success.

In a corporate environment all business goals need to have a 'v' shape in the back of them!

What do we mean by that? Well imagine a line management structure where the Manager at each level has a set of goals to achieve and a goal sheet on which they are written. That goals sheet is shaped like a dart at the front with the tail cut out into a 'v' shape at the back.

Now imagine that the guy at the top of the line management structure has a 'v' shape cut out of the back of his or her goal sheet. This cut out is for the pointed bit of the next guy down's 'dart' to fit into and so on and so on down the levels.

The powerful thing about this concept is that it involves team work and of course to use the hackneyed phrase, TEAM means 'together everyone achieves more.' So the business goals of everyone in the line management team structure are co-dependant and interlinked and focused on the achievement of the single overall corporate goal of the team.

This process generates vast leverage because the collective power of the team is concentrated in a specific direction, whereas in an organisation whose Managers do not understand the principles and benefits of goal setting, or whose goals do not contribute to the overall goal, cannot possibly hope to achieve the same results as those achieved by goal leveraged organisation.

Imagine a very tall lady wearing stiletto heels…imagine the concentration of weight pressure per square centimetre over the surface area of those tiny heels, then compare this pressure with that of the same lady who this time is wearing wellington boots!

Corporate linked goals create the concentrated stiletto heel effect.

Collaborative interconnected goals are essential if the organisation is to reach its full potential and this is fair and equitable because the organisation more easily reaches *it's* goals when everyone reaches theirs, and so everyone shares in the benefits.

Businesses like the John Lewis Partnership Retail Group are a particularly good example of this because they don't have employees, they have partners and every partner knows that when John Lewis hits *its* numbers *they* will get a significant reward. This inspires those who work there to do their level best to make sure they achieve best possible, an attitude that is in stark contrast to other retailers who merely pay a wage.

Anyway, collective goal setting is not the purpose of this chapter, and it has been mentioned here merely to illustrate the awesome power of this process!

What we really need to talk about are goals for *you*.

We all have a choice; we can be wondering generalities in life, or meaningful specifics. In other words we can live our lives like a ship without a rudder drifting helplessly and aimlessly at the mercy of the wind and tide to finish up 'somewhere,' most probably a wreck on the beach of life.

OR.

We can use those same winds to drive us forward in the direction of our desired destination.

Without goals you are as pointless as a broken pencil!

Note from Nancy: John vividly remembers hearing at a seminar he attended on goal setting many, many, many, many years ago, that a long term study carried out by a leading US University revealed that only 3% of MBAs had written down goals…and that this group earned *ten times as much* as the other 97% combined.

Taking that on board, we would be rather foolish to ignore the benefits of having written down goals!

However, just how do written down goals potentially enable such tremendous results to be achieved?

Let's consider Sir Edmund Hillary, or to give him the full honours, Sir Edmund Percival Hillary KG ONZ KBE. (20 July 1919 – 11 January 2008) We bet nobody called *him* Percy!

Anyway, he was a New Zealand mountaineer who, on 29 May 1953, along with one Tenzing Norgay, became the first climbers confirmed as having reached the summit of Mount Everest.

What has this to do with goal setting?

Well let's imagine this wild idea…Imagine Sir Ed was out on holiday in the Himalayas, when one morning, bright and early, he and his wife Louise were out for a pre-breakfast stroll when on rounding a corner, the full majesty of Mount Everest came into view towering high into the sky.

Sir Ed screeches to a halt and admires this awe inspiring sight, then he turns to Louise and says, 'I think I'll pop out after breakfast and scale that blighter, should be home before it gets dark darling!'

We don't think so!

First he set the goal: To climb Everest and the year and date that the climb would begin, allowing for the weather.

Next he would have had to plan his route, then his base camp and then the camps spaced out all the way to the summit. He would have had to plan (there's that word!) the logistics of how he was going to get the supplies to each camp, what supplies he would need, the man power he would need etc. It was going to be a massive undertaking, that when accomplished was going to be a World first: To be the first man on Earth to climb Everest!

Planning and goal setting are irrevocably linked, in fact most goals of any significance are going to take a great deal of planning in order to achieve.

Once the goal has been set, we must focus our efforts on achieving it, we must keep our goal before us constantly like a guiding light. It might be a picture of the goal; a car or a house or some other tangible asset. It might be a card with the goal written down, either way we need to be reminded of it morning, noon and night.

A powerful dynamic of the goal and goal setting process is that it keeps us focussed and prevents us shooting off at a tangent and wasting precious time, it keeps us focussed so when someone calls us and asks us to do such and such, we can quickly think, 'If I do this will it get me any nearer my goal or will it push my goal further away?'

If it's the latter you may consider that you must say '*No thanks!*'

As we set off to pursue our goal, it is inevitable that we will meet roadblocks. If we had no goal then the roadblock would stop us and as we had no particular purpose, we'd just turn round and go back the way we came.

With a goal worth striving for, we would go round, under, over or through the roadblock in order to keep on track to achieve the goal.

Imagine for a moment you've planned a family weekend to the beach! Car's packed, kids are tied in the back, wife has her magazines in the front and you, Dad, are in command at the wheel and off you go.

After an hour on the motorway you glance in your rear view mirror and catch sight of flashing blue lights way back in the distance. You instinctively glance down to check your speed…great, 73mph, you're ok, it's not you!

You tell the kids there's a police car coming and they both turn to watch it speed by, and then…the overhead gantry flashes up a warning, the motorway is closed by an accident 17 miles ahead, brake lights are coming on in the distance and the traffic grinds to a halt!

So what do you do?

'Sorry kids, the road's blocked up ahead, it's going to take hours to get past the accident, so we'd better go home and forget all about the beach.'

I can imagine what would happen next! The kids would wail fit to drown out the police sirens and your wife would set about you big time, 'I knew it, you never wanted to go on this weekend away, now you've got the perfect excuse to go fishing with Ernie tomorrow, which is what you wanted to do all along!'

Don't think so!

You would pacify the kids, you'd see how far the next junction was, you'd play 'I Spy with my little eye,' and you would find a way round the roadblock so you could still achieve your goal.

To create any kind of meaningful result your goals must inspire you, in fact a goal could be referred to as a dream that you want to accomplish, and that reminds us of a recent Skype conversation John had with Gargi Rastogi, the father of a special young man called Ash, for short. Gargi runs a factory in Thailand and during the Skype session he dropped out this little winner, which we give you here.

'A dream does not allow you to sleep!'

What he meant was that when a dream or goal becomes so powerful that it prevents you from sleeping. It *must* be achieved and you can never rest until it is and because of this it will eventually be *yours*!

IN CONCLUSION

The trip across the plain of your career can be long and arduous and even terminal for some because they will never make it, not because they didn't necessarily have the innate ability, but because they were unwilling to change failure habits for success habits and were also unwilling to change themselves in order to 'become' what they were capable of becoming.

Something like the fat guy who claims he wants to be slim trim and sexy but still eats burgers by the dozen. Reality for him is that he didn't want it seriously enough to actually go through the pain of slimming down to achieve his goal...he just didn't want it badly enough.

This is the reason we spent so long talking about default settings and governments in power, because if these aren't right, then you will never be able to succeed for all the reasons we discussed.

Something else in passing.

Nobody slops into success, success comes to those who spend their time in the performance zone. This is where the action is, this is where things happen, this is where you shine as the best of the best, ahead of all the rest, because you do whatever it takes to be a winner!

The fact of the matter is that in order to succeed, we must first get ourselves 'right' and then work to create and develop that highly motivated 'dream team,' so that *together* you can succeed at the highest level.

It is a very true statement that success is a journey not a destination, a journey during which those who succeed are typified by those who invest in themselves by buying books to enrich their minds with success principles, rather than have their brains sucked out by inane TV shows or equally inane 'bad news' newspapers. Far better to read a book to expand your mind, or turn your journey to work into an 'open university' situation, where through your headphones, you can devour audio books and learn during what would otherwise be unproductive time.

Once more, it is a true statement that leaders are readers and also audio book listeners!

Just a rider to add on that subject however; never make *gaining* knowledge the objective, because you can have all the knowledge in the World, but unless you *apply* it, it will be of no use to you at all.

There are many stones still left unturned on all the topics in this book, and if we were to attempt to address them all in detail, then this book would be as big as Tolstoy's 'War and Peace.'

What we can offer is a help and advice contact that you can plug into simply be e-mailing us your questions and queries. In addition to this you can also join our inner circle, which is a community dedicated to success and it is here that the real leaders associate with us on line, so we can help, guide and steer their progress across 'the plains' to Success Mountain.

We never wish our children 'good luck' as they undertake something new because we know that 'luck' has nothing to do with achieving success, so we won't wish you good luck either!

Finally, let us remind you of some things:

Did you know that there is nothing new in the World?

Think about this from William Shakespeare written 400 years ago…

'Our doubts are traitors and make us lose the good we oft might win by fearing to attempt.'

Or along the same lines, from a more modern source, Karim Seddiki, 'Doubt kills more dreams than failure ever will.'

If you don't start, you can't finish, so start and never stop. Never stop growing and becoming, never stop striving for your lofty goals because they are there to be achieved.

Victory does not always go to the strongest man, it goes to the man who thinks he can.

Remember, you are better than you think you are...Here's to your success!

■■

PERSONAL MESSAGE FROM JOHN AND NANCY

It is quite possible that you have never previously come across some of the more esoteric concepts described in this book and we accept that some of the information is hard to grasp and possibly even harder to believe!

Understanding and implementing these concepts is essential to your success and so to help you, we have a dedicated e-mail address through which you can contact us to ask for clarification and further guidance should you need it. You can also apply to join our Inner Circle, its free and as a member you will be able to access more help and information.

You may have a business concept that has come to you fresh from the Universe and would feel a little more confident about it if you could gain some expert advice, or even some funding to get it started, again we can help.

Nancy and I are quite prepared to offer our readers free, unbiased advice and ongoing support in complete confidence to help each one of you reach and climb 'Success Mountain.'

If you would like some help, just drop us an e-mail to: class4action@gmail.com

We promise to respond within 5 days.

John & Nancy